CULTURE SMART!

UAE

John Walsh

·K·U·P·E·R·A·R·D·

First published in Great Britain 2008
by Kuperard, an imprint of Bravo Ltd
59 Hutton Grove, London N12 8DS
Tel: +44 (0) 20 8446 2440 Fax: +44 (0) 20 8446 2441
www.culturesmartguides.com
Inquiries: sales@kuperard.co.uk

Culture Smart! is a registered trademark of Bravo Ltd

Distributed in the United States and Canada
by Random House Distribution Services
1745 Broadway, New York, NY 10019
Tel: +1 (212) 572-2844 Fax: +1 (212) 572-4961
Inquiries: csorders@randomhouse.com

Series Editor Geoffrey Chesler
Design Bobby Birchall

ISBN 978 1 85733 451 7

British Library Cataloguing in Publication Data
A CIP catalogue entry for this book is available from the
British Library

Printed in Malaysia

This book is available for special discounts for bulk purchases for
sales promotions or premiums. Special editions, including
personalized covers, excerpts of existing books, and corporate
imprints, can be created in large quantities for special needs.

For more information in the U.S.A. write to Special
Markets/Premium Sales, 1745 Broadway, MD 6–2, New York,
NY 10019 or e-mail specialmarkets@randomhouse.com.

In the United Kingdom contact Kuperard publishers at the
above address.

Cover image: The Burj El-Arab hotel, Dubai. *iStockphoto*
The images on pages 13, 16, 35, 52, 99, 103, and 107 are reproduced by permission
of Rustom Vickers.
Images on pages 42 © soylentgreen, 67 © Qatari, 76 © Matson, 78 and 106
© Bruno Girin, 125 © Máth Dávid, 127 © ghaya alghaya, 152 © iStockphoto

CultureSmart!Consulting and **Culture Smart!** guides have both
contributed to and featured regularly in the weekly travel program
"Fast Track" on BBC World TV.

About the Author

JOHN WALSH is Assistant Professor in Marketing and Communication at Shinawatra University in Bangkok, Thailand. His doctorate, from the University of Oxford, was for research on international management. He has written extensively for learned journals, contributed to number of encyclopedias, undertaken media and consultancy work, and also been widely published in non-academic fields. Having lived and worked in Sudan, Greece, South Korea, Australia, and the United Arab Emirates, he now lives in Bangkok with his wife and daughter.

Other Countries in the Culture Smart! Series

- Argentina
- Australia
- Austria
- Belgium
- Botswana
- Brazil
- Britain
- Canada
- Chile
- China
- Costa Rica
- Cuba
- Czech Republic
- Denmark
- Egypt
- Estonia
- Finland
- France
- Germany

- Greece
- Guatemala
- Hong Kong
- Hungary
- India
- Indonesia
- Ireland
- Israel
- Italy
- Japan
- Kenya
- Korea
- Libya
- Lithuania
- Mexico
- Morocco
- Netherlands
- New Zealand
- Norway

- Panama
- Peru
- Philippines
- Poland
- Portugal
- Romania
- Russia
- Singapore
- South Africa
- Spain
- Sweden
- Switzerland
- Thailand
- Turkey
- Ukraine
- USA
- Vietnam

Other titles are in preparation. For more information, contact: info@kuperard.co.uk

The publishers would like to thank **CultureSmart!**Consulting for its help in researching and developing the concept for this series.

contents

contents

Map of UAE

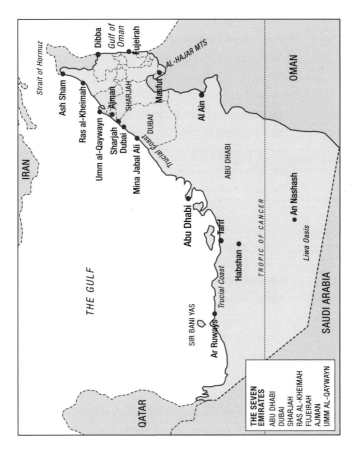

introduction

The United Arab Emirates is at once one of the most conservative societies in the world and one of the most forward-looking. Only a generation ago it was a very poor desert country on the peripheries of the Arab world and Britain's colonial empire. The discovery of oil changed all that, although it took the wise leadership of Sheikh Zayed bin Sultan al-Nahyan to ensure that the blessing of wealth did not become a curse. He aimed to balance tradition and modernity, and the UAE today is a country of contrasts, embracing luxurious hotels and shopping centers while its black-*abaya*- and *shayla*-clad women are mostly kept securely out of sight.

The UAE aims to be one of the focal points for the Arab world in international relations and a global leader in media and electronic commerce. Yet it intends to do that while maintaining its own social systems and networks, and while slowly integrating its women into public life as much as possible commensurate with its core social beliefs.

Dubai has become one of the most popular and fashionable resorts for affluent travelers. Sharjah is a center for cricket in the Middle East. The greening of the desert is a long-term project that has required hundreds of thousands of migrant workers to develop the infrastructure. Now there are new industries ready to take their place alongside oil and gas. The banking, media, and asset management sectors are vibrant and technologically advanced. Yet the UAE retains its Islamic essence, and the daily routine of life is accompanied by the cadences of the muezzin's calls to prayer, in the shade of the many mosques.

Traveling to or living in the UAE can be a challenge. It is likely to involve moving beyond your cultural comfort zone but, having made the effort to bridge the divide, you will find people whose embrace of modernity is exhilarating and whose effort to combine the ancient and the modern is a fascinating example of globalization. Combined with the legendary Arabic sense of hospitality and generosity, this makes the UAE a potentially extremely rewarding place to visit. This book will introduce you to the history and culture of the Emiratis, tell you what to embrace and what to avoid, and smooth your path toward full enjoyment of a fascinating experience.

Because place and personal names from the UAE are transliterated from Arabic in a variety of ways, the most common forms have been used here, at the risk of some minor inconsistencies.

Key Facts

Official Name	United Arab Emirates (Al Imarat al Arabiyah al Muttahidah)	Member of the Gulf Cooperation Council, Organization of Petroleum Exporting Countries
Capital City	Abu Dhabi	Pop. approx. 1.2 million
Main Cities	Dubai, Abu Dhabi, Sharjah	
Population	4,440,000 (est.)	Growth rate of 4% per annum
Ethnic Makeup	20% Emirati, 50% South Asians, 22% Arabs and Iranians, 8% others, incl. Westerners	Varies according to demand for migrant labor
Age Structure	0-14: 21% 15-64: 78% 65: 1%	73% of the adult (15+) population is male.
Area	32,278 sq. miles (83,600 sq. km)	
Geography	Located on northern coast of Arabian Peninsula along the coast of the Persian Gulf. Bordered by Saudi Arabia and Oman	Composed of seven individual Emirates: Abu Dhabi, Dubai, Sharjah, Fujeirah, Ajman, Ras al-Kheimah, and Umm al-Qaywayn
Terrain	Mostly desert, with rolling dunes and generally flat apart from eastern mountains	
Climate	Desert climate, hot and humid on coast	
Natural Resources	Petroleum, natural gas	Less than 4% of land is suitable for agriculture.

Currency	Emirati dirham (AED) US $ = 3.67 AED (May 2007)	
Language	Arabic. English is widely understood.	Migrant labor communities have their own languages.
Religion	Islam is the state religion: 96% of population is Muslim, mostly Sunni, but 16% are Shi'a	Christian Churches may be found. Other religions are generally tolerated but practitioners should be discreet.
Government	Federation of Seven Emirates	Powers divided between Federal and Emirate level governments
Media	All Emirates have at least one state-controlled TV station, and several satellite stations offer different packages. Both English- and Arabic-language radio stations are available. The media are controlled to prevent broadcast of inappropriate or indecent material.	In addition to Emirate-based papers, national newspapers published in Dubai include the Arabic-language *Al Bayan*, *Al Khaleej*, and *Al Ittihad*, as well as English-language papers *Gulf News*, *The Gulf Today*, and *Khaleej Times*.
Electricity	220/240 volts, 50 Hz	Three-prong plugs are used.
DVD/Video	DVD PAL, Region 2	
Telephone	The UAE's country code is 971.	Dialing out: 00 + country code
Time Zone	GMT + 4 hours	No daylight saving time

chapter one

LAND & PEOPLE

GEOGRAPHY

The UAE is located on the northern part of the
Arabian Peninsula, and lies along the Persian
Gulf. The land itself is mostly flat and, away from
the coastline, almost entirely desert in the interior.
To the east, the border with Oman is marked by
the elevated ground of the Al-Hajar Mountains,
which rise to a maximum of around 6,500 feet
(around 2,000 meters), while to the south and
west, the border with Saudi Arabia is arbitrary—
that is, it does not follow any particular obvious
geographical feature. To the west are the small
Gulf States of Qatar and Bahrain, while Iran lies
across the other side of the Persian Gulf. A
number of small islands are located in the Gulf
and controversy occasionally flares with Iran over
the ownership of three of these in particular.

There are no natural harbors along the UAE
coastline and the two that are principally used are
man-made. The waters are quite rich in fish and
marine life and it is possible to see whales and

sharks, in addition to edible fish such as mackerel and tuna. Although these days meat is imported in large amounts, historically fish represented the major form of protein for Emirati people, supplemented by the occasional lamb or goat.

There are some oases within the interior of the country, notably at Al Ain. These areas offer a little variety in terms of vegetation and wildlife. Al Ain is famous for its mangoes, for example, while alfalfa and date palms are also grown—dates come into all Emirati meals in one form or another. However, away from these areas, most of the country is uninhabited. This does not mean that it is devoid of life, because the desert actually offers quite a variety of flora and fauna for those who know where to look. Nevertheless, it

remains a dangerous place to travel and visitors should not attempt to travel alone or without informing people of where and when they are going.

Recently, the Abu Dhabi government has taken the initiative of planting many thousands of mangrove trees and these represent a new habitat for species that have not been seen in the UAE before.

The seven Emirates that make up the UAE are Abu Dhabi, Dubai, Sharjah, Ras al-Kheimah, Fujeirah, Ajman, and Umm al-Qaywayn. Abu Dhabi is the largest Emirate geographically and also its waters contain the majority of the oil and gas deposits that have so radically transformed Emirati life and society. Dubai is the commercial center of the country, while Sharjah is the center of the limited manufacturing base. The other Emirates tend to be regarded as less attractive than these, and are much less visited by tourists, for example.

CLIMATE

The climate of the UAE is principally hot and dry, reaching up to 109°F (43°C) on the coast and 115°F (46°C) in the interior. However, the January temperature is a much more manageable 64° Fahrenheit (18°C). Desert nights can be cool, but only in the deeper interior does this really have any noticeable impact. Average annual rainfall is approximately 3.9 to 5.9 inches (100 to 150 mm), but this is subject to considerable variation, which makes agricultural management even more difficult. During the winter, the temperature ranges somewhere between 50° and 75°F (between 10° and 24°C), and this is considered the most pleasant time of the year to visit. There is even some fog on rare winter mornings, although this burns off quickly. However, irrespective of the lack of rainfall, the UAE experiences up to 100 percent humidity all year-round, which makes living there almost impossible without air-conditioning. Prior to the arrival of electricity, people survived by living in certain caves that offered breezes to ameliorate the humidity.

The Shamal is a wind that blows constantly in June and July at a speed of generally just under 31 mph (50 kph). The winds originate in Pakistan and blow from the north through Iraq and Iran, often causing extensive sandstorms. It is advisable to stay indoors if sandstorms blow up.

THE PEOPLE

Apart from the oasis city of Al Ain, the majority of the people live in the coastal cities or the suburban areas surrounding them. Since agriculture is so difficult, the number of people living in the countryside is very limited. The oil industry does require some people to live in other remote locations.

Approximately 80 percent of the population are non-Emirati citizens. Exact population statistics are quite difficult to ascertain because so many of the population are migrant workers who move backward and forward according to the demand for labor. Most of the non-Emirati population are Asian, with large cohorts from India, Sri Lanka, Pakistan, and Afghanistan. The great majority of these workers are male, and they tend to be recruited on an ethnic basis according to the type of work required. Smaller proportions come from East Asian countries and are also generally funneled toward specific jobs. These workers tend to contain more women than the South Asian contingent. Generally, people have been recruited to work at a lower level than their qualifications would normally justify. There is another professional

group of people who work in managerial and technical occupations and who may be recruited from Western countries, South Asia, and Arab countries, particularly Egypt and Iran.

When considering the Emiratis themselves, the concept of ethnicity is not seen as relevant, and is not discussed. Everyone who was present within the borders of the country when independence was declared in 1971, or who had a suitably strong familial connection to a recognized citizen, was unilaterally accorded citizenship and, in return, was expected to renounce any previous political affiliations. Don't risk causing offense by bringing up this subject. While many women have been imported as wives from neighboring countries and others have joined the body of citizens, all are Emiratis, and there is no need for debate. The same situation happened in Ras al-Kheimah when it joined the UAE in 1972.

It is often reported that Emirati women are expected to wear the full *abaya* (body-covering black robe) and *shayla* (head and sometimes face-covering black shawl) because of the presence of so many male workers, who are separated from their own women and who therefore represent a potential threat to their honor. But it is not certain that this is the case.

A BRIEF HISTORY

In common with other Islamic societies, the Emirati people are not as interested in the pre-Islamic period as in that afterward. Consequently, the archaeological and literary evidence that exists to help illuminate the past has not been as strongly examined as might have been the case. Some historical issues arouse a measure of controversy, especially when Western archaeologists or historians postulate hypotheses or present evidence that is held to be contradictory to some traditional beliefs. However, it does appear that, in the remote past, Arabia as a whole had a climate with greater rainfall than it does now and agriculture was a much more viable activity. The tips of the peninsula, in what are now Oman and Yemen, which enjoy the benefits of the Indian Ocean monsoon system, boasted rich cultures with dams and irrigation dating back to 2000 BCE. This was because the dry climate of Arabia seems to have stabilized in its current nature around five thousand years ago. Since that period and probably before, a mixture of different peoples have entered into and passed through the peninsula, and some stayed to share their culture. Cultural institutions seem to have spread to the UAE

region from Africa, Iran, and the north. It is not now believed that a single Arabian people hailing from the peninsula was the origin of the current population. Eratosthenes, a Greek writer of the third century BCE, writes of Yemen, known as Eudaimon Arabia, as having four distinct ethnic groups.

Trade flowed through Arabia from important centers, such as Mecca, from early times, and settlements from the Roman period show evidence of exchange of goods. Frankincense, an important trade good, was carried to Gaza and on to Europe. Eastward, trade routes had been established for thousands of years. Spices from the remote Indonesian islands have been found in the Syrian desert and dated to 2000 BCE, and at least one route passed through the desert, possibly utilizing territory now in the UAE. The most important state in Arabia at this time was Saba, known in the west as Sheba, with its capital at Ma'rib. However, it is clear that a number of other smaller states existed and, from time to time, a king with pretensions to become known as a "unifier" emerged. It was more common, though, for tribes to live together in a state of autonomy. These tribes did not necessarily have a common ethnicity but instead represented a group of communities living in close proximity to each other, peaceably, and open to the outside world. Inscriptions and archaeological data reveal that the region was in contact with the Mediterranean states, Egypt, India, and cultures further afield.

In the centuries before the conquest of eastern Arabia by the Sassanian dynasty of southwestern Iran, the area of the UAE witnessed the growth of local communities, crafts, coinage, and the development of language. The horse was first used at some period during the three centuries BCE. The Sassanians were dominant for five centuries before the religious message from the Prophet Mohammed reached the people of the Gulf Coast. They had recently become aware of Christianity through contacts with distant lands, and there appears to have been a variety of religious beliefs held by the people. Nestorian Christians built a monastery in Sir Bani Yas. However, the Islamic message soon overwhelmed other forms of belief. In 630 CE, the first emissaries arrived from the Prophet Mohammed, and conversion to Islam occurred very swiftly. The death of the Prophet led to a rebellion against the religion he had brought, but this was soon destroyed and Islam began to be exported overseas, using the base at Juffar to invade Iran and begin the conversion of the Iranian people.

The export of Islam was extremely successful over the next centuries. Enormous amounts of booty were taken as part of military campaigns and it is likely that some portion of these goods made their way back to the Gulf Coast. Muslim courts of the period generally benefited from the wisdom of Islamic scholars and artists, and most rulers were patrons of art and culture. The standard of living in Islamic cities was among the highest in the world. However, different dynasties varied in their willingness to comply with this model and some rulers held more tyrannical ideas. The lives of the people of the future UAE continued to depend upon the commerce provided by the sea and the nature of powerful neighboring rulers. The extent to which states with their power bases on the coast or on oases could exert their influence over the nomadic Bedouin tribes of the interior was limited because it was so difficult to travel there and to force people to abide by their laws.

In due course, European powers came to prominence in the Gulf as they sent out fleets to create colonies and improve trade with distant places. The first to arrive in force were the Portuguese, who were motivated by the desire for trade.  Dismayed by the strong hold on trade maintained by Muslims wherever they went, they blockaded the ports in the Persian Gulf and elsewhere. This resulted in severe damage to many Muslim economies, including Arabia and the coastal region. The opportunities for piracy had been available in the Gulf for some centuries, but the presence of enemies with a different religion multiplied the possibilities. The Qawasin pirate sheikhs created the Emirate of Ash-Shariqa, now known as Sharjah, and it served as a base for pirate ships operating in the Gulf and beyond.

In the sixteenth century, the Ottoman Turkish Empire succeeded the Egyptian Mamelukes as

the preeminent Middle
Eastern power, and
Ottoman ships became
active in the Gulf. The
Ottomans did not govern
Arabia directly, and a
number of autonomous
and semiautonomous sheikhs and emirs
retained control of their local power bases.

Since much of Arabia is desert, there was
usually nothing but empty space between the
cities and oases. In this space, nomadic Bedouin
tribes were able to move about more or less
freely. They came into contact with the settled
peoples when it came to trade, when they were
wanted as mercenaries, or when their paths
crossed with those making the Hajj pilgrimage
to Mecca. There was a great deal of civil war and
conflict within Arabia across the centuries, and
a variety of religious schisms also caused
divisions. One of the more important of these
was the development of the puritanical Wahhabi
tradition in central Arabia in the eighteenth
century, which subsequently became extremely
influential in Saudi Arabia and whose influence
extends across the border to the UAE. The
majority of people on the Gulf Coast have

continued to adhere to the "well-trodden path," or *Sunnah*, and are described as Sunnis. However, they do not as a rule take this form of belief to the extreme that Wahhabi believers do. Both consider themselves proper Sunnis. Islam has generally been a tolerant religion and, throughout history, people of different beliefs have quite happily lived in the same communities. In more modern times, this tolerance has become strained for various political reasons and it has become necessary for tolerance to be encouraged or enforced through various social mechanisms.

The Wahhabis waxed in power and maintained military strongholds in the center of the peninsula. By the beginning of the nineteenth century, Wahhabi power had become so great that the Ottoman leaders decided to take decisive military action against them. This resulted in the Ottoman occupation of western Arabia, but acceptance of Wahhabi dominance was recognized on the Gulf Coast. As Wahhabi rulers coalesced to create the Kingdom of Saudi Arabia, the Gulf Coast states retained political independence as Emirates, to some extent because they were focused on the sea rather than the land.

The Al-Qawasin pirate sheikhs had skirmished with the British for some time as their control of India intensified. In due course, the British inflicted a naval defeat on the Qawasin fleet in 1819, which led to the decline in power of that dynasty. Replacing the Qawasin power base was the Banu Yas tribal confederation, in which the Abu Dhabi Emirate was dominant. This confederation was centered on the Abu Dhabi oases and was land based rather than maritime in nature. The al-Nahyan faction, which principally derived from the Al Bu Falah tribe, rose to become the dominant force in coastal politics.

Three treaties helped establish the UAE as a discrete state. The first was a peace treaty among the tribes, signed in 1820. The second was the 1853 treaty that established perpetual peace at sea and that led to the name Trucial Coast being affixed to the Emirates. The third treaty, signed in 1892, restricted the Trucial States and their foreign relations entirely to the discretion of the British state. The Trucial Coast then became known as the Trucial

States and continued to include Bahrain and Qatar as part of the combined States. This name remained in use until independence from Britain was finally established in the twentieth century.

This period was marked by the attraction of immigrants, from India, Iran, and other countries, who could see the opportunities for trading in the new city of Dubai and the presence of international trade routes. While the British overlords largely ignored the States, providing such legal infrastructure as was necessary, migrants and indigenous people forged their own, individual culture based on trading and the desert.

In the 1930s, the global depression was partly responsible for the collapse of the natural pearl markets, but this itself heralded the signing of contracts by the emirs of Dubai, Sharjah, and Abu Dhabi for exploration for oil in Trucial States territory. However, it was not until 1962 that oil from Abu Dhabi became the first to be exported from the county. By this time, from 1952, the Trucial States had established a semiannual council, the forerunner of the FSC (described below). In 1968, the

British announced the withdrawal of all forces from the Persian Gulf by the end of 1971, and this stimulated negotiations among Trucial States leaders as to the formation of a state and its nature and shape.

Negotiations were complex, and in 1971, when independence was achieved, both Bahrain and Qatar decided to establish independent states, while Abu Dhabi, Dubai, Sharjah, Fujeirah, Ajman, and Umm al-Qaywayn agreed to form the United Arab Emirates. The next year, Ras al-Kheimah opted to join the UAE, having initially been reluctant to do so. The first president of the UAE was Sheikh Zayed bin Sultan al-Nahyan, who was subsequently reelected to the post on five-year terms by the rulers of the individual Emirates.

MODERN TIMES

Income from oil exports continued to grow, especially after the increases in oil prices in the 1970s. In the early part of the decade, the price of oil quadrupled as the Organization of Petroleum Exporting Countries (OPEC), of which the UAE was a member, took advantage of the rapid expansion of economic development around the world and the accompanying increase in demand for oil. This increase, which caused a dramatic realignment of global political power and influence, was also closely related to the issue of Arab–Israel relations, since the majority of OPEC members were Islamic countries from the Middle East. The ability of the UAE government to bring about the economic and social development of the country was thereby greatly enhanced.

The long building boom that was sparked has continued until the present day and, as management of the economy leads to its becoming more diversified and complex, seems set to continue for the foreseeable future. However, this was possible only because of national unity, which was far from assured in the early 1970s. Dubai and Ras al-Kheimah in particular were resistant to federal control of their individual affairs. Centralization of the state was led by Sheikh Zayed, and the crucial breakthrough occurred when Sheikh Rashed of Dubai agreed to become prime minister and vice president of the UAE in 1979, signaling the end of Dubai's resistance to the process of federalization. Ras al-Kheimah, meanwhile, has become largely marginalized in political terms as Abu Dhabi oil money has come to finance most of the state and subsidize the lives of those

UAE citizens who live in Emirates without oil resources of their own.

Foreign relations have been characterized by a pro-Arab and a pro-Western stance. The UAE has favored diplomacy and financial support to its neighbors as a means of maintaining peace and security in the region, and this has at least succeeded in keeping the peace at home. The principal threat to the country's security has come with controversy over the ownership of several islands in the Persian Gulf, which are also claimed by Iran. Clearly, ownership of these apparently trivial islands in the oil-rich Gulf is important because of the oil surrounding and beneath them. At the time of the creation of the UAE, Iran landed troops on Greater and Lesser Tunb and on the mainland in Sharjah and Ras al-Kheimah. They subsequently withdrew in the face of international opposition, but have not renounced their claim.

Meanwhile, the UAE demonstrated its commitment to the maintenance of national borders by making help available to the forces liberating Kuwait in 1990–1. The country also sent troops to Kosovo in 1999 as UN peacekeepers. The state has also been involved in supporting the reconstruction of Iraq following the removal of the Saddam Hussein regime.

SHEIKH ZAYED

Sheikh Zayed bin Sultan al-Nahyan was the first president and visionary leader of the UAE, from its inception in 1971 to his death in 2004. His understanding of the developmental needs of his people was astonishingly perceptive and has revolutionized what was in living memory

an economically undeveloped coastal strip of land with few apparent resources. Sheikh Zayed was born some time around 1918— birth dates were not then recorded or considered important—in Abu Dhabi. The youngest of four sons, he soon distinguished himself by his willingness to learn about the lives of his people, from the pearl fishers to the Bedouin tribes, from whom he developed a passion for falconry. He first took a leadership role in 1946, when he was appointed to govern the oasis villages of Al Ain and the adjoining desert region. From this post he developed his administrative skills and deepened his knowledge of the people of the desert and their culture, beliefs, and aspirations. One particularly important result of this was his appreciation of the importance of women in communities in which resources were scarce, and their role in holding those families and communities together. As a leader, Sheikh Zayed was also characterized by his desire to bring the fruits of development to all the inhabitants of his country and to ensure that everyone could participate in that development. In this, he was often confronted by those with more conservative views about women and their role in society.

In 1966, Sheikh Zayed succeeded his elder brother as ruler of Abu Dhabi and, with the support of his family, pushed forward his plans for development. He increased contributions from Abu Dhabi to the Trucial States Development Fund as a means of enabling all Emiratis to profit from its oil wealth. At the same time, he was determined to preserve the ways and culture of his people, and he introduced enduring initiatives aimed at educating young people into traditional ways of life. Looking both to the past and to the future, Sheikh Zayed achieved great things for his people, as can be seen by comparing the development and progress of the UAE with that of some other states that have also benefited from the presence of oil reserves.

GOVERNMENT AND POLITICS

The UAE is a federation in which the seven individual Emirates retain certain powers for themselves while a federal government oversees state-level policy, such as foreign affairs and defense. On the death of the founding father and president Zayed bin Sultan al-Nahyan, the

presidency passed to the next ruler of Abu Dhabi, President Khalifa bin Zayed al-Nahyan. He is assisted by Vice President and Prime Minister Sheikh Muhammad bin Rashed al-Maktum of Dubai, who succeeded his brother Sheikh Maktum bin Rashed al-Maktum on his death in 2006. The two al-Maktum brothers are well-known for their extensive horse-racing interests.

The highest authority in the land is the Federal Supreme Council (FSC), which is composed of the seven leaders of the individual Emirates and which meets on a quarterly basis to decide high-level issues. The FSC voted unanimously for the posts of president and vice president, and it is common for such a show of unity to be made in such cases. The emirs of Abu Dhabi and of Dubai are recognized as the most important members of the FSC, and they can veto decisions if necessary;

however, emirs prefer there to be a show of unity, and any controversial decisions are customarily settled in private, one way or another.

Historically, Arab rulers have appointed advisors to serve as part of their council in an institution known as a *majlis*, which is also a physical space in which consultations and debates take place. The name of the parliament or Federal National Council (FNC) is the Majlis al-Ittihad, which continues this tradition. The FNC has forty members, half appointed by the individual emirs and half chosen by election. To become a member of the Electoral College, it is necessary to be appointed by an emir. Only Electoral College members are eligible either to be candidates or to vote in the election. There are fewer than seven thousand members of the College, although this includes more than a thousand women, and a female candidate from Abu Dhabi became the first to claim a seat in the FNC. Voting intentions are influenced by tribal and familial links as well as policy stances, although the extent to which the former or the latter predominate varies on a person-by-person basis. The FNC is permitted to review policy and comment upon it, but has no power to amend it or to introduce legislation independently.

According to UAE citizens and government, there is no need for political parties or leaders, since all necessary debate takes place through the FSC and Majlis or FNC. If political parties were to come into being, it is likely that there would be some pressure to create parties based on religious beliefs, and this could prove divisive. Religious extremism has a glamour that appeals to some people, and the state is determined to suppress it and is anxious about its potential influence.

The laws are upheld by judges appointed by the president. Individual Emirates have their own courts to deal with civil, criminal, and commercial cases, as well as Islamic courts to administer cases involving family or moral issues. Abu Dhabi, Sharjah, Umm al-Qaywayn, Ajman, and Fujeirah have established a federal-level justice system for cases deemed appropriate, and it is hoped that Dubai and Ras al-Kheimah will in due course join this system.

The UAE is a full member of a range of international organizations, including the International Monetary Fund (IMF), the International Labor Organization (ILO), the Group of 77 (G-77), the United Nations (UN), and the Organization of Petroleum Exporting Countries (OPEC). The UAE is also a member of the Gulf Cooperation Council (GCC), alongside

Qatar, Kuwait, Bahrain, Oman, and Saudi Arabia, which was formed in 1981. The GCC has proven itself to be an effective forum for diplomacy, but has been less successful in stimulating mutual economic development aside from the oil and gas industry.

THE EMIRATES

Emiratis are very conscious of their home Emirate and are usually very strongly attached to their home ground. Since the UAE has come to be dominated economically and politically by Abu Dhabi, and Dubai in particular, the visitor can run the risk of forgetting that the other Emirates exist at all. This would be a pity for many reasons, not least of which is that each one has something special to offer.

SEVEN EMIRATES

Abu Dhabi 28,209 sq. miles (73,060 sq. km.) Pop. c. 800,000	The largest and richest Emirate. It is Abu Dhabi's oil wealth that has developed the whole country. Abu Dhabi can also be the most conservative socially.
Ajman 100 sq. miles (260 sq. km.) Pop. c. 50,000	The smallest Emirate and now almost entirely urbanized, joining with neighbors Sharjah and Dubai as a potential megacity.
Dubai 1,583 sq. miles (4,100 sq. km.) Pop. c. 1,400,000	Dubai city occupies a large part of this Emirate, which derives its wealth from Jebel Ali Free Trade Zone, advanced service businesses, and tourism.
Fujeirah 444 sq. miles (1,150 sq. km.) Pop. c. 130,000	Fujeirah is almost totally mountainous, and its limited economy is based on rock crushing supplemented by state subsidies.
Sharjah 1,004 sq. miles (2,600 sq. km.) Pop. c. 640,000	Sharjah is the home of most of the UAE's limited manufacturing capability. It has a 5,000-year history of early settlements.
Ras al-Kheimah 656 sq. miles (1,700 sq. km.) Pop.c. 120,000	Ras al-Kheimah consists of two separate pieces of land. For most of its history, Ras al-Kheimah was part of the Ash-Shariqah Emirate (Sharjah) and was ruled by the Qawasin pirate sheikhs.
Umm al-Qaywayn 301 sq. miles (780 sq. km.) Pop. c. 27,000	Umm al-Qaywayn was also part of Ash-Shariqah, and its economy was based on both piracy and pearl diving.

Population figures are necessarily estimates, as accurate figures are not easily available at lower than the national level, while the numbers of migrant workers moving into and out of the country are constantly changing.

THE ECONOMY

The economy of the UAE depends almost entirely upon the presence of offshore oil and gas. It is estimated that Abu Dhabi, in the territory of  which the bulk of the reserves are located, has about 10 percent of all the world's known reserves. The oil and gas are extracted by a variety of joint ventures between UAE government oil companies together with large foreign oil companies. The foreign companies provide technical and technological competence, in general terms, while the local partners can offer access to the oil fields. Both sides have made a great deal of profit and will continue to do so for the foreseeable future. No one knows exactly how much oil is left in the world because new finds are still being made, although these are generally smaller than those that have already been discovered. Additionally, improvements in extraction technology mean that in the future it will be profitable to extract oil from difficult areas that currently are an unprofitable proposition. The best estimates seem to suggest that there are around a hundred to a hundred and twenty years' worth of oil reserves in the world, given current rates of extraction.

It seems likely that the moment of peak production of oil has already been passed, meaning that current and future oil extraction will be lower than in the past. However, this will not mean the end of the UAE and its current economic boom. Approximately 40 percent of all oil revenues are reinvested through the Abu Dhabi Investment Authority (ADIA) in strategic industries and investment projects that will yield sustainable profits in the future—for example, hotels, airports, and high-value real estate. It is rumored that even if the oil revenues were to stop immediately, the investments that have already been made and the profits flowing from them are sufficient to ensure that no Emirati citizen need ever work again. Whether or not this is true is difficult to ascertain because the ADIA is reluctant to discuss these matters publicly, for obvious reasons.

The impact and benefits of the oil money are present in every aspect of UAE society. Oil keeps fuel and energy prices low and enables bright lights to keep burning—the lights that illuminate the highway from Abu Dhabi to Dubai shine so brightly in the desert air that they are one of the very few man-made items to be visible from space. Enormous shopping centers are luxuriously appointed and air-conditioned, and are full of shops that would find energy and rental costs crippling in nearly any other country. Emirati citizens have their energy and telephone costs heavily subsidized, and all costs for business are kept at a low level.

Dhow Trade

The Dubai Creek runs through the center of the city of Dubai. It is a place where people like to gather to stroll along or drink coffee while watching the boats coming in to land and the ferries chugging their way back and forth across the water. The cargo boats are dhows, forms of the one-masted trading vessels used by Arabs for centuries to carry goods up and down the coasts of the Arab, African, and Indian worlds. Most dhows these days come from across the Gulf from Iran, but some come from further away. Their cargoes now consist of locally produced vegetables, fruit, rice, and cereals imported into the UAE, as well as cotton goods and low-cost manufactured items mostly from India and, increasingly China, and more high-tech products such as air conditioners, microwaves, and media players from South Korea, Taiwan, and Japan. This modern form of the Silk Route shows the reality of globalization in action.

The UAE government maintains a light hand on the economy, and it is usually not difficult for foreign investors to establish their businesses. Investors mostly appreciate this laissez-faire attitude, although it is not always so popular among the workers who have little hope of welfare payments or of appeal against unfair employers. Indeed, migrant workers without a job or a valid work permit are obliged to leave the country within forty-eight hours.

Locally owned businesses or businesses in partnership with foreign interests that are particularly successful include banking and hotel management. These industries have the advantages that there is local demand and that the ability to establish and manage a business successfully can be profitably exported overseas by opening international branches. The UAE business community has identified its sustainable competitive advantages as being ownership of capital (they are cash rich) and ability to manage large-scale enterprises. Their lives contrast with those of the majority of the population, whose most common interactions with business are via grocery shops and supermarkets, private schools and clinics, and the *souks* and markets in which everyday items are to be found. The UAE is essentially a dual economy, in which two separate systems coexist with each other, with people being dependent on members of the other sector but rarely coming into personal contact with them. Having said which, there is a definite entrepreneurial sector of UAE society, which, whether working for the government or on their own account, are committed to creating and developing new business structures. Having capital behind them does help, but personal attributes are also proving important.

The UAE government has initiated an offset program to help develop its infrastructure. When foreign companies want to make an investment in the country, they may be asked also to build an additional institution or facility to demonstrate goodwill. This can include development of the educational, commercial, and military sectors. Few foreign companies find this an onerous requirement because their opportunities for profit are high and long-term investment will bring long-term gain. However, it does inhibit the presence of investment projects in which profits are likely to be low, as in the case of basic manufacturing or service industries, apart from those that are small enough not to attract any such requirement.

As nearly all inputs, including labor, need to be imported for a manufacturing facility to be established, there is little prospect of manufacturing becoming an important part of the economy. However, the generous designation of free trade zones and high-level transportation and distribution systems offer many possibilities for future investment in highly value-added industrial sectors, such as infrastructure, health care, tourism, and entertainment. The government of Dubai has provided the Dubai Internet City and the Dubai Media City high-technology industrial parks, among others, to stimulate investment in knowledge- and information-based industries that they anticipate represent the future of the state's development.

Although it may well be possible for Emirati citizens to look forward to a life of leisure, the government is acutely aware of the dangers of an

underemployed but affluent workforce. It intends to provide incentives for its people to work, based on stimulating and challenging employment, opportunities for self-advancement, and an awareness of the need of the nation to become a leading light in the Arab world. In doing so, it is also required to negotiate with the traditional nature of its society, its attitudes toward work, and its attitudes toward women in the workplace.

THE THREAT OF TERRORISM

The UAE has firmly positioned itself as an ally of the developed Western nations. Its members are strongly committed to their Islamic beliefs and traditions, but do not see this as an obstacle to becoming a modern and sophisticated society. They are prepared to take steps to make sure that their security and reputation are not threatened by terrorist violence. If this includes surveillance or the use of secret police, then they will trust their rulers to manage this for the good of the country as a whole. Of course, it takes only one person to perpetrate an outrage, but the authorities will be doing their best to ensure that this never happens. Security issues or the ways that this is ensured are not considered to be joking matters.

chapter two

VALUES & ATTITUDES

There are three principal factors that combine to create the values and attitudes of Emirati people. The first of these is Islam; the second is Arab and Bedouin tradition and the life of the desert; the third has developed much more recently and is based on the presence of money and power.

Islam is one of the world's greatest religions and, owing in part to its proximity to the sacred cities of Mecca and Medina, the UAE has been suffused with its influence for much more than a thousand years. Arab and Bedouin traditions are, in some respects, even more venerable than the religious influences. The life of the desert meant often intense competition for scarce resources and the separation of family units and tribal groupings from other communities by difficult terrain. This inspired the creation of elaborate and vital rules for hospitality and a protocol for negotiation and trade that has been maintained until the present day. The third factor has reinforced the social or conceptual distance between Emirati people and outsiders.

Emiratis generally define themselves in terms of their family or tribe first of all, Emirate second, country third, and Arab world fourth. Not everyone thinks this way—well, not everyone thinks about this issue at all. However, all parts of this identity seem to be important, and visitors should treat them seriously. The government is making considerable efforts to promote the nation as the basis of personal identity and this is bearing some fruit. Nevertheless, old loyalties disappear very slowly.

When wealth is more or less equally distributed, social relations between people are conducted on a generally equitable basis. However, now that Emirati people are much wealthier than the more numerous migrant workers in their country, they have become accustomed to consider foreigners to be, at least to some extent, employees who might represent a threat of some sort. The presence of so many male migrant workers has led to the tighter segregation of Emirati women and so more social occasions have become off-limits to visitors to the country. As a result, it has become more difficult for an outsider to become truly integrated into Emirati society, to feel a genuine part of it, and to understand its various dynamics.

STATUS AND SOCIAL STRUCTURE

One adage that Emiratis occasionally use is "to be as clever as an Egyptian." In common with the people of most countries, foreigners are often met with preconceptions about their role and status in society based on broad ethnic generalization. Consequently, Iranians and Iraqis are expected to be professionals, Afghans laborers, and Indians business managers. Since most people are generally quite open and tolerant of other people, it is quite possible to break through this initial stereotype, but there are occasions when this can be problematic. In any case, visitors should be aware that, based on where they come from and what they look like, there will be some expectations of what kind of person they are, what kind of work they will do, and, consequently, some measure of their status in society. Emirati society is quite conservative socially, so attempting to shock or startle people by presenting them with unexpected appearance or attitudes is likely to meet with disappointing results.

Moving from being an outsider to an insider is likely to be a lengthy process, requiring persistence and perseverance, without the presence of some kind of personal or family connection that could short-circuit the time required. Those who are able to achieve this will find that there are numerous subtle, often unstated and longstanding, distinctions in status within Emirati society. The family, which is related to the tribe, remains the basic social structure and, no matter how far members may roam, they will always be aware of their roots in the familial home. This sense of belonging is likely these days to have been reinforced by the building of substantial housing areas (compounds full of buildings are not really suitably described as "houses"), which anchor the family even more deeply into the land.

Relations between different families, within and across different Emirates, are affected by events and agreements that may have taken place years previously. Without learning a great deal about family history—rather more than an outsider can reasonably hope to do—it is extremely difficult to determine why people behave they way that they do. Understanding this will at least enable the visitor to appreciate that there is a reason that some kinds of social interaction, ranging from parties to networking functions to business partnerships, work better than others, even if he or she may not realize exactly what factors are involved or how long ago they may have come into play.

ARAB PRIDE

Emiratis consider themselves Arabs and are proud of their heritage. It was the Arabs who were blessed to receive the Prophet Mohammed and, hence, the message known as the Islamic religion. This was delivered to Mohammed by the Angel Gabriel in the Arabic language, which is believed to be the language of heaven. Inspired by this message, Arab armies conquered and in due course inspired the conversion to Islam of people from Spain in the west to Indonesia in the east, via all the many countries and peoples in between. Temporal Arab states and empires occupied enormous areas of land and endured for centuries in some cases. The Ottoman Empire, for example, conquered the Christian stronghold of Byzantium, threatened Vienna, and held all of Europe to ransom. Many of the powerful states of the Steppes, including the Mongols and Tamburlaine's hordes, were or became Muslims as a result of their influence. This is a proud and very distinguished heritage, with which people identify. Arabs and other Muslims may be different ethnically, but the shared memory of their Islamic past is a badge of pride that unites them.

The tide of history had changed by the twentieth century, however, and Arabs and

Muslims generally were subjected to the depredations of Western colonialism. The humiliation that people felt as a result of being colonized was intensified when it became clear just what reserves of oil were available to those who controlled their territories. Arabs often draw a parallel between British control of the oil fields prior to the Second World War and the American-led invasion of Iraq, which appears to many people to be for the same motivation.

Clearly, there is scope for enormous levels of very heated debate about these issues, in which the role of Israel is customarily involved as well. Visitors would do well to bear in mind the history of misery and exploitation, on top of ancient victories and glory, that their Arab friends and colleagues will bring to their side of any debate. In the UAE such discussions are somewhat different, in that Emiratis control the economy and the power within most social forms of interaction and it is, at the very least, polite to listen to what one's hosts have to say.

SOCIAL NETWORKS

Extensive although frequently opaque social and familial relationships underscore a great deal of Emirati life. Marriages between suitable members of different families are one of the most common means of extending these social networks, although there are other means as well.

Islam places a great deal of stress on charity, and there are many charitable foundations that exist to collect donations and redistribute them to the needy. These organizations represent new opportunities for people to join together and establish new relationships or strengthen existing ones. Some business concerns also operate in the same way, although only for those Emiratis who adopt a hands-on attitude toward managing the business.

RELIGION

The religion of the UAE is Islam. Islam came into being through the words and actions of the Prophet Mohammed, who was active in the Arabian Peninsula in the seventh century AD. According to Islamic belief, Mohammed was visited by the Angel Gabriel, who recited to him the holy word of God, which was subsequently written down and became known as the Koran. God's intention was for Mohammed to be the final in the succession of prophets who had been sent to Earth, including Adam, Noah, Abraham, Moses, and Jesus, among others, all of whom are revered as holy prophets in their own right. However, as the final prophet, the message of Mohammed superseded all the others and, consequently, the Koran explains exactly how humans should live. The term "Islam" itself literally means "submission," and Muslims believe that they are submitting themselves constantly and continually to the will of God.

Mohammed's message was rapidly spread throughout neighboring areas, reaching eventually from the Atlantic Ocean abutting North Africa to the remote Indonesian islands in the East. Large areas of Iran, India, central Asia, and the Steppes were among the other regions in which people were converted to Islam, partly by the sword and partly through religious revelation.

Islam combines within itself both the spiritual realm and the temporal realm, and consequently many, although not all, Muslims believe that the rulers of countries should be religious leaders, not politicians or nonreligious leaders. The leadership of the UAE has to date managed to keep separate the two realms and, as a result, governed the state through political perspectives, notwithstanding the need for religious solidarity and the pursuit of ethical policies.

THE FIVE PILLARS OF ISLAM

The Five Pillars of Islam represent the very foundations of the religion and provide structure to the daily life of Muslims.

• The first is the Shahadah, or profession of faith. This is the belief that there is no God but Allah and Mohammed is His Prophet. Making this profession categorizes a person as a member of the Muslim community.

• The second pillar is the five-times-daily prayers. All Muslims must listen out for the muezzin who will issue the call to prayer on five occasions each day. This is the signal for the faithful to wash themselves and pray in the prescribed way. These

occasions are difficult to miss in most parts of the UAE, because so many people have wished to demonstrate their faith and return something to society by sponsoring the building of a new mosque that there are now numerous muezzins who give the call in close proximity to each other. In mosques, women and men have separate sections. If it is not convenient for the person to visit a mosque for prayers, then people (men) may line up their prayer mats so that they are facing Mecca and make their prayers. Visitors should note that the prayers cannot be completed if a woman is in view or walks in front of the praying men.

- The third pillar of Islam is the tax of *zakat*, or purification, which is levied at up to 10 percent of an individual's assets at the end of the year. Charitable giving is a strong part of Emirati society and it is inspired by this foundation of the religion. It might be noted that Islamic thought considers the paying of interest on money lent to be a sin. This has given rise to the many Islamic banks now to be found in the UAE, which offer a variety of schemes such as co-ownership of assets to avoid the sin of paying interest.

- The fourth pillar is fasting during the monthlong period of Ramadan. Muslims should refrain from refreshments to the body during daylight hours.

- The final pillar is the requirement to go on the Hajj, which is the pilgrimage to Mecca. These days, the proximity of the UAE to Mecca and the transportation links make this a much less onerous trip than it once was and so nearly everyone is able to make the Hajj at least once. Many Emiratis in any case have relatives across the border in the Kingdom of Saudi Arabia and may visit them quite often.

Muslims always accompany the mention of the name of the Prophet Mohammed with the words "Peace Be Upon Him" (which may be seen abbreviated in English as PBUH). Generally, Islamic thought precludes the representation of human beings in any form of art, as this would be disrespectful to God's work in creating the original people. In particular, there is a very strong taboo accompanying the portrayal of Mohammed. Recently, cartoons representing the Prophet led to angry demonstrations around the world and death threats. As a visitor, do not let the Western or skeptical perspective of using humor to describe religion overcome you in the UAE.

ATTITUDES TOWARD WOMEN

Emiratis are, in common with many other Muslim people, proud of the way that they respect and protect their women; however, the way that this is manifested is very different from how many other cultures believe women should be treated. According to a combination of Koranic and traditional beliefs, Emiratis believe that men and women should be kept separate from each other most of the time. This is because they will be tempted into sins of improper intimacy if they are allowed to be together. To prevent this from happening, the best solution is to keep women covered up, to hide their physical shape, and, in most cases, secluded from public view.

Previously—before the current generation, when oil wealth began to transform the country—women more commonly worked outside the house and were not required to cover their bodies to the extent that they now are. According to some Emiratis—and this is an issue that is controversial and consequently only approached very carefully—it was the presence of so many male migrant workers that persuaded Emirati men to insist that the women of their families protect themselves by wearing the *abaya* and *shayla*. There is very little incontrovertible evidence for this issue either way and, given the sensitivity of the subject, there are few opportunities to discover the truth, even if it is considered important.

The result is that, in the twenty-first century, Emiratis generally believe that they respect and protect their women much better than people from other cultures do. Indeed, it will generally be clearly protested by people of either gender that this is the best means of regulating society and inspiring people to be virtuous that there is.

Some Emiratis who have international education or experience or some other means of influencing their thinking may be willing to consider other methods, but it would not be considered acceptable to talk about such a thing within the country. However, family leaders both male and female are almost entirely strongly in support, in public, of the current system at its basic level of maintaining women's purity. There may be a big difference between public and private speech.

Sheikh Zayed recognized and understood this feeling among his people and promoted social stability within the country. At the same time, he held the vision that it would be necessary to integrate at least some women into the labor market in order to provide positive role models for the many capable Emirati women who wished to work outside the household. Achieving this was a long-term goal, which necessitated the creation of workplaces and jobs in which women could  perform without exposing themselves to possible danger or criticism. Slowly, this is happening and some integration is taking place. However, not every family or individual agrees and so the progress is gradual and by no means irreversible in many cases.

For foreigners, it should be understood that men and women will almost certainly be treated very differently. Men can walk about and do more or less what they will. Women face a very different situation. A man in the same place as a woman to whom he is not directly related or married will find himself subject to restriction, but women are free to move about in public only with a suitable chaperone. A single women is likely to encounter difficulties if she wishes to visit a restaurant or shopping mall alone, join an exercise or social club or, sometimes, drive a car or walk down a public street. This does not happen all the time, but abuse may be encountered, or police or other security personnel may wish to question the woman concerned. This is usually an unpleasant or intimidating experience at best, and may result in detention at worst. Considering these possibilities, most women are advised to walk in public cautiously in terms of dress and attitude, and to be accompanied by other people, preferably men, who may reasonably be held to be their legitimate chaperones.

Clearly, this is very different from the practice in Western countries. Whatever attitude a person has toward visiting or living in the UAE, it is always advisable to dress and behave in public in ways that will be considered respectable. Aside from any serious interaction with the authorities, dressing modestly and appropriately result in obviously better service than dressing in what is considered to be a disrespectful way. The same is true, of course, for many other countries and societies.

Muslim Emirati men are free to marry non-Muslim women, although only if they are "people of the book"—Christians or Jews, who are part of the same Abrahamic religious tradition. A wife in these circumstances will convert to Islam if she wishes to live in the UAE. However, the reverse is not true, and a marriage between a Muslim woman and a non-Muslim man who does not convert to Islam is not recognized, and those involved are subject to arrest for fornication.

In the event of a marital breakdown, it will be assumed as a matter of course that children will be assigned to the care of the father. In the case of a cross-border marriage, where the couple has been living in a country that does not follow Shariah (religious) law, this may not comply with local law, and on breakdown of the marriage there are reports of children having been "kidnapped" by the father or someone operating on his behalf. In these cases, UAE Shariah law will support the

father, and this can make access to children for
the mother very problematic.

Islamic law in the UAE permits polygamy, with
men permitted to marry up to four wives, as long
as each is treated equally. It is increasingly
common for a man to have a single wife. Emirati
men who marry Emirati women receive a
generous grant from the government for doing
so, as a means of promoting social cohesion.

INSHA'ALLAH

"*Insha'allah*" is one of the most commonly heard
phrases throughout the Arab world. It means "If
God wills," and is used on any occasion when the
future is concerned. To the Muslim mind,
everything that happens is in the hands of God
(Allah) and so it would be presumptuous of a
mere human being to claim that what will
happen depends principally on his or her own
efforts. This sometimes upsets Westerners who
do not understand the emphasis that is placed
upon the word. It may sound as if "*Insha'allah*"
is used to indicate that something will only
happen if God takes a direct interest in doing it.
However, this is not the case. It means instead
that the individual will seek to perform whatever
commitment has been made but it must be

borne in mind that God might have other plans, in which case it will not be possible for the individual to complete the task.

BACKHAND ECONOMY

Many large business deals are conducted in an opaque fashion, especially those related to defense and security areas. Rumors often circulate about whether under-the-table payments may have influenced one deal or another. These rumors are fed by the lack of information available about the decision-making processes involved. This lack of transparency suffuses the business culture of the UAE—and not just the UAE—which is combined with the patronage culture in which one individual takes care of the interests and affairs of his extended family. These factors, combined with the high level of importance attached to family ties, mean that there are powerful forces that contribute toward the taking of shortcuts in business. People wish to do favors for each other and to protect the interests of their families and connections and, in such societies, decisions are made that cannot be easily explained to outsiders not privy to knowledge of the basis of the decision.

Additionally, there are also some open cases of fraud and corruption in the country, no doubt prompted by the enormous amounts of money that might be involved.

WASTA

Wasta is an Arabic word meaning something like "influence" or "connections." It is a concept relating to the degree of connectedness that an individual may have with other people and organizations and, hence, the ability of that individual to get things done. In common with people of many other societies, Emiratis prefer to do business with people whom they know and trust. Since the process of getting to know and trust another person can be time-consuming and even expensive, it is better and more efficient if people can somehow short-circuit this process by pointing to some kind of tie or connection with another person that can act as a symbol of trust and friendship.

Membership of the same family or tribe is perhaps the most powerful symbol of this instant connection; one Emirati introduced to another family member will immediately understand that the long years of relationships established across the generations mean the individual can be trusted, since actions are guaranteed by elder members of the family or tribe. The general position is that trust of this sort is automatically offered to a family member in this way, but that does not mean that it cannot be lost in severe circumstances. Bearing in mind that households can be quite large, if four wives have six or eight or more children each, then it is clear that powerful taboos will develop to ensure harmony at the household level. Sometimes, of course, it is necessary to expel a person who is damaging that harmony in a way that cannot otherwise be managed.

So, the concept of *wasta* comes from a perfectly understandable and rational source, even if it does not always work out that way in practice. What it means in reality is that some people, who have *wasta*, are given privileged access to scarce resources that other people cannot have. The scarce resources include the time and attention of important people and officials. Consequently, the *wasta*-holders get their business attended to more swiftly than those without, and this can be construed as unfair and even corrupt. It is certainly true that there are people who base their career on their possession of *wasta* and their ability, therefore, to complete paperwork and have decisions approved above and beyond what another person, although perfectly entitled to receive these benefits, cannot manage. Be that as it may, people wishing to do business with a UAE business or its government will customarily seek to equip themselves with allies with high levels of *wasta* to facilitate their business.

TOLERANCE AND PREJUDICE

Emirati people are proud of their heritage and their country, not to mention their society and culture. This is perfectly understandable, but they can occasionally be dismissive of other cultures and societies that differ from theirs. However, most Emiratis will be far too polite ever to bring this up in conversation unless the other person is being particularly pushy. The Arab concept of hospitality is very strong in the UAE, and this generally extends to all kinds of social interaction. One person will act as the host for all the others, and Emiratis are generally practiced at taking this role.

One area of conversation that is generally best avoided concerns religion and politics and, in particular, the role and nature of Israel and its supporters. Although there are plenty of far-sighted Emiratis with a mature appreciation of global politics, there are plenty more who hold prejudices that may lead to inflammatory argument, and this would be very impolite. Protests against supposed Israeli crimes or sins flare up from time to time and are passionately supported. Visitors should be very cautious about these displays of powerful emotions or political controversy. Polite visitors will not antagonize their hosts by disagreeing with them about matters that are held to be so self-evidently true.

In other cases, people show the kinds of prejudices, common around the world, that derive from lack of knowledge and experience. Bearing in mind how restricted the lifestyles of many women in particular can be, it is not surprising that they might have accumulated mistaken notions about how people from other cultures and societies think and behave, for example, "all Americans behave like harlots." Such ideas might well have been fed by television or other media, and these in turn shaped by beliefs not held by visitors.

SENSE OF HUMOR
Emiratis are able to access media from most countries of the world, subject to suitability on religious and ethical grounds. Consequently,

they have been exposed to the globalizing influence of the spread of mass media and this has had an impact upon their own sense of humor. Social conservatism in the UAE means that there are enormous areas of society and culture that are off-limits for humor, and these are areas that provide significant amounts of material for humor and satire in Western countries. Emirati humor therefore often concentrates on stereotypes or physical humor that may appear unsophisticated to the visitor who is not able to appreciate the subtleties within them: these may be quite daring, while contriving to appear wholly innocent. Such performances are mostly imported from overseas. Emiratis enjoy laughing as much as anyone else, but they have to exercise some care as to when to allow their humor to show in public, and even in private.

chapter three

CUSTOMS & TRADITIONS

Customs and traditions are important to Emiratis, seemingly even more so because of the comparatively short period in which they have crystallized in their present forms. Feasting and celebration in the past, even a generation ago, was quite a different affair from what it is today. Materialism has become a central part of celebrations as people wish to demonstrate their generosity and treat their friends and family to the good things of the world. Of course, not everyone is enamored of this change and many, especially among the ranks of the elderly and the more spiritually concerned, feel that the real message of the various celebrations is being compromised.

A number of the traditions of the past have certainly been transformed and even reinvented for the modern age. Falconry and horsemanship, for example, were skills necessary for survival in a difficult environment in the past, but have now become rather glamorous celebrations of a semi-mythical past rather different from its reality.

Again, it is quite a common phenomenon for societies to re-create their past so that it appears to be rather more convivial than it might really have been. For a visitor to the UAE, therefore, when it is possible to gain access to the performance of a custom or tradition, and many family-based occasions will probably be closed, care should be taken to try to identify and appreciate the original contours of the event and not dismiss the whole thing as razzmatazz with little intrinsic meaning.

Falconry

Falconry has been a part of Bedouin life for centuries. The sharp-eyed birds of prey can see potential victims from an enormous distance away and have proved themselves to be useful and valuable companions in the desert. Falcons now are trained to retrieve targets flung into the far distance and to return to the arm of their handlers. Sheikh Zayed developed a deep passion for falconry when he was living among his desert-dwelling people, and this passion has helped the practice to survive and flourish.

CALENDARS

The UAE follows the standard Islamic calendar. The calendar is based on the lunar cycle and there are twelve such months in each year, which amounts to about 354 days per year. The first year of the calendar is that which is marked by the *hijra*, in which the Prophet Mohammed traveled from Mecca to Medina. This occurred, in the Western calendar, in the year 570. For example the year 2007, according to the Islamic calendar, is 1428 AH (After the *Hijra*). Most official documents are dated according to the Islamic calendar, although it is also common to use a dual system.

One issue that does have an impact on the lives of visitors to the UAE is the nomination of Thursday and Friday as weekend days off. This is because Friday is the most holy day of the week for Muslims. Muslims pray five days a week and there is no specific requirement to attend additional services on a Friday. However, it is quite common for people to attend a mosque on a Friday morning or lunchtime in order to listen to a sermon from a favored Imam. In other countries, such a sermon can be the starting point for a demonstration or rally in favor of some political or social issue, but this has not been the case in the UAE, especially since monitoring of what Imams say takes place and controversy is not encouraged.

Having weekends on Thursday and Friday causes some difficulties when trying to do business with organizations from countries in which Saturday and Sunday are recognized as days of rest. It means that the only days during the week in which people from both countries will be scheduled for work are Mondays, Tuesdays, and Wednesdays. This can be problematic when dealing with situations that require urgent attention. As a result, it is becoming more common, especially in Dubai, for weekends to be nominated as Friday and Saturday, to provide an additional day of joint work on Thursdays.

RELIGIOUS HOLIDAYS
Ramadan

Ramadan is one of the most important times of the year for the people of the UAE and it has many impacts upon life in the culture. For Muslims, Ramadan is the yearly period of fasting that culminates in the feast of Eid Al-Fitr. Fasting is an important part of being a practicing Muslim and it has the benefits of concentrating the mind on the spiritual sphere, as well as promoting self-discipline. During this time, which occupies the ninth month of the lunar calendar and, hence, varies from year to year according to the Western calendar, Muslims will refrain from drinking or eating or smoking or any kind of sexual activity during the hours of daylight. Traditionally, the fast ends daily when, if two threads are held aloft, one black and one white, they cannot be distinguished. This is then succeeded by a period of feasting on nearly every night, as the Emirati people take the opportunity to celebrate another day with their friends and families, taking turns to entertain each other.

Ramadan has a strong impact upon working life, since hours of work may be adjusted to reduce stress for the people observing Ramadan. In any case, many people feel tired and drained during the day and, consequently, their level of work and judgment may dip during this period. The only people generally permitted not to fast are small children and pregnant women, although medical necessities may also waive the obligation. Children are usually permitted to stay awake until quite late at night in order to enjoy the celebrations and this can make them sleepy and fractious during the daytime. There is little to be gained by criticizing this arrangement as the fast is one of the Five Pillars of Islam, and is a tradition that is strongly upheld and welcomed. Many people will spend the daylight hours concentrating on religious issues, praying and reading the Koran more than usual. Questioning this is likely to cause offense.

Eid al-Fitr

Eid al-Fitr, which marks the end of Ramadan, is the largest and most important festival in the UAE. Over the course of several days, Emiratis will organize extensive feasts to entertain their families and friends. Traditional meals will be assembled, including barbecued lambs and large dishes of pilaf rice. The intense spirituality of the festival, together with the draining effects of Ramadan and the effects of the feasting all together, tends to cause most of the business of the country to slow down or even stop for a few days. Don't expect much progress, if any, to be made in business terms during this period.

It should also be borne in mind that, although technically the restrictions on eating during daytime do not apply to non-Muslim people, it is at best impolite and at worst offensive to flaunt this fact in front of people who are fasting in very high temperatures. Causing offense is always to be avoided, of course, and the visitor will find this is facilitated by the fact that most restaurants will be closed during the daytime anyway. In

multinational organizations, most employers
will provide closed rooms where people may
eat during the daytime without calling
attention to themselves.

Other Religious Holidays

In addition to Eid al-Fitr, Emiratis also
celebrate the holiday of Eid al-Adha, which is
known as the festival of sacrifice. During this
holiday, Muslim people will recall the sacrifices
made by Abraham, notably when he was asked
by God to sacrifice his own son, although once
Abraham demonstrated his obedience, God
provided a substitute in the form of a ram.
People will sacrifice an animal on this day,
generally a lamb, which is then used as the basis
of a feast. Customarily, a third of the meat of
the animal is eaten by those present, a third is
given away to friends, and the remaining third
is donated to the poor.

The two Eid festivals move in date from year
to year because they are based on observations of
the moon. There has in the past been some
controversy concerning sighting of the moon
when imams at one mosque can view the moon
on a different day from an imam in another
mosque. Consequently, although holy days are
announced in advance, it is best to await

confirmation closer to the day before making any definite plans.

Two other holy days that are celebrated in the UAE are the Mouloud and the Leilat al-Meiraj. The first of these commemorates the birth of the Prophet Mohammed and the second his ascension into heaven when, upon reaching spiritual perfection, he was taken into heaven by God.

Given the presence of people from around the world working in the UAE, it is not surprising that nearly every religious festival is celebrated in some form or another. Work schedules will not usually be changed to cater to these festivals—Christmas Day, for example, is usually scheduled as a regular working day. People who wish to celebrate their own special religious occasions will generally do so discreetly for, although religious tolerance is well ingrained in the country, it is possible to cause offense to people who may be unprepared for what this entails. For example, people who consider themselves very tolerant can become upset if another religious calendar dictates celebration on a day of Islamic penance or vice versa. In the same way, Christmas cards for Christian people featuring the Virgin Mary may be considered very irreligious and, in those shops where they may be found, they are kept under a pile of other cards, so as to avoid notice.

Hindus, Buddhists, and Sikhs are among those who practice their observances in private homes and are not disturbed. Religious observances within a personal residence will not be disturbed.

NATIONAL HOLIDAYS

There are two new year celebrations in the UAE, one of which represents the start of the Islamic New Year and which varies according to the sighting of the moon, and the other is the Western New Year, which is fixed on January 1. In recent years, these two holidays have taken place quite close together, although this will not always be the case. The UAE's National Day is celebrated on December 2 each year.

OTHER CELEBRATIONS

Family occasions such as marriages and birthdays are also opportunities to reestablish and reaffirm social relationships and are, consequently, popular occasions for celebration.

Informal celebrations are also likely to break out in response to important sporting, social, or political events. Winning a big football game, for

Sword Dancing

The *ayyalah al-ardha* is one of the traditional sword dances performed by men living in the UAE. To drums and percussion beats they leap between the blades, showing their virtuosity and skill while, on occasions, being cheered on by the *na'asheet*, the female performers sanctioned to perform this entertainment. The sword dance is customary at weddings and other celebrations, and is remembered as part of the desert tradition of living brought into the twenty-first century.

example, is likely to inspire a procession of cars tooting their horns, with riders leaning out of windows waving scarves and flags and cheering. On occasions of spontaneous celebration such as this, those who are fortunate enough to have access to Emirati women's quarters may hear the famous ululation.

It might be noted that funerals do not have the same qualities of coming together and reinforcing social relationships that the happier family occasions do. They tend to be much more low-key affairs and the deceased is, according to tradition, buried secretly in the desert while wrapped in a simple white sheet. Funerals are not usually the occasion for the mass gathering of relatives and friends that is found in other Middle Eastern societies, partly because there are so many other opportunities these days for such gatherings. Mourning tends to take place in private rather than in public, although there are exceptions to this.

LOCAL CUSTOMS AND FOLKLORE

The two great traditions of Emirati society, the desert and the sea, have both inspired many stories and legends. These have been told and retold around campfires for generations. Common heroes include the men so generous that they sold their last few possessions to feed their guests and hence were reduced to absolute poverty, as well as the clever fellows who adapted to overseas life and the slings and arrows of

fortune, like Aladdin. Another important figure is the servant who is also the leader: this is a person who seems to hold a lowly position but whose wisdom and streetwise ability can guide emirs and generals on to the desired path. This figure is very common in Bedouin culture and, of course, offers the opportunity of success and glory even to the poorest individual through proper behavior.

Folk wisdom in the UAE can date from the very remote past, even to the pre-Islamic period, and as a result it may occasionally be frowned upon when it might appear to contradict religious beliefs. However, Emiratis, as well as their government, do respect and honor their past heritage and want to preserve those parts of it that they can. Some traditions clearly come from other countries and cultures because of the UAE's coastal position and location on various trade routes. Ancient Mesopotamian influences in pottery making, for example, may be seen in archaeological finds in the area. However, these cultural influences have also been mediated or seen through the prism of local, Emirati perspectives and beliefs. Over the course of centuries, therefore, distinctive and unique forms of cultural expression and folk wisdom have been brought into being. This includes the building of boats, the use of folk medicine, and the creation of poetry to express beliefs and ideas that may be

characteristically Emirati in nature. The late Sheikh
Zayed observed that a country that did not know
its past had neither present nor future. Maintaining
knowledge and appreciation of the past and
allowing this to guide development of both society
and economy in the future is an important part of
the charge the Sheikh laid upon his government.
Various museums and cultural centers help to
remind people of the past. The Museum at Ajman

is one notable
example of how life
was lived in the past.
Observing the
architecture of the
forts and the new
and old *souks* is
another avenue for
appreciating local
knowledge and the ways of adapting international
ideas to local circumstances.

The smaller Emirates tend to have retained
more of a feeling of the past than many parts of
Abu Dhabi and Dubai, in particular, which have
been almost entirely rebuilt in modern and
modernistic styles. Folk wisdom also persists in
the household, and in this case it can be difficult
for the visitor to access. Consequently, the
wisdom is often most conveniently found when

re-created or represented by foreigners acting out the part of Emiratis of the past.

Poetry

Writing poetry is one of the most noble activities in which a man can engage. It ranks alongside horsemanship and falconry in demonstrating manliness, sensitivity, and understanding of the cultural heritage. Neighboring Iran has for centuries had a tradition of poetic epic, and this has perhaps helped the native Bedouin spinning of tales around the campfire to become elevated into a high form of art. Although it would not be seemly to dwell on romantic love, Emirati poets might reflect on their place in the universe and in society and on matters of spirituality.

In the modern UAE, Arab poets compete to win televised contests for prizes worth millions of dollars. As more and more money is being poured into preserving and reviving Emirati culture, the promotion of Emirati and Arab poetry is likely to make it much better known in international circles and help further to position the UAE within the leading group of globalizing nations.

chapter four

MAKING FRIENDS

Friendship is a very important part of Emirati society, as it is in most parts of the Arab world. Owing to social attitudes, friendship is almost wholly regulated along gender lines, and there are very few circumstances in which a man and a woman can be friends with each other without provoking a scandal. Friendship is generally intensified by either prolonged proximity or joint membership of some social group or family. It is not impossible to achieve these means of entering circles, but it is difficult, since foreigners rarely find themselves as part of the same social, sporting, or business circles as Emiratis. However, it is possible to have established a friendship with an Emirati who has been studying overseas, or through a mutual interest, such as football or camel racing.

As we have seen, the religious, historical, and managerial implications of being an Emirati tend to mean that establishing a genuine relationship with an outsider on a more or less equal basis is unlikely. Still, working together in an organization is probably the most common way of establishing the level of trust that is required to break through the barriers that separate people. Of course, those visitors to the UAE who have similar cultural backgrounds to Emirati people will find it easier to establish a social relationship but, even so, true friendship may prove to be elusive. This is usually because the Emirati will have a different view of friendship from the visitor, especially if the visitor is not familiar with friendship and hospitality patterns in the country.

Friendship is taken very seriously by Emiratis, and it represents a serious commitment in terms of time and honesty. Once a relationship is established, which takes longer than is common in Western societies, it can hardly ever be reversed (on the other hand, that makes enmities very severe). Some Emiratis have become disenchanted with visitors who seem at first to be open and friendly—which would demonstrate a definite commitment to friendship—but who then seem to back off on later meetings. If friendship is desired, then people should make real efforts to ensure that they carry through with the commitment.

ATTITUDES TOWARD FOREIGNERS

As mentioned elsewhere, Emiratis are both very hospitable and welcoming and also prone to ascribing certain characteristics to foreigners based on their country of origin. The level of understanding of that country is likely to vary quite considerably, and the visitor may be subject to comparison with stereotypes. This, while not likely to be intentionally insulting, may be at least disconcerting; for example, not all American women behave like Britney Spears, and not all British men wear bowler hats.

As in many countries, people with white skin often receive more respectful treatment than people with black skin when first encountered. Given this situation, many of the migrant workers in the country prefer to emphasize their position in society by relying on their professional status rather than their own personality. However, it should also be noted that, increasingly and at a rapid rate, the UAE is becoming a globalized and cosmopolitan society, and its members may have considerable experience of the world and the different people who live in it. Knowledge and experience lead toward tolerance here as anywhere else. Those visitors who are Muslims are more likely to feel that they are being accepted into a larger family in which all are more or less equal in the face of God. Islam insists that all Muslim men and women are treated as equal, and there is a long tradition of Arab and Islamic culture in which this has taken place.

The tendency to stereotype foreigners is often exacerbated when it comes to women, especially women who are walking alone in the streets or in some other public place. Women doing this may, depending on their ethnicity, receive unwanted advances or comments. Notwithstanding the desire to demonstrate equality and independence that women may feel and wish to express, it is often the case that prudence makes life a great deal easier.

GREETINGS

The Arabic language is used in a formal way in many situations in the UAE. Many aspects of social relationships have been formalized, and greetings are one of those areas in which varying from protocol would be considered strange and impolite. The Arabic greeting universally employed, "*Salaam Aleikum*," has the sense of "May peace be with you," and the proper response is very similar, "*Wa Aleikum as-Salaam*." This is used in face-to-face communication and also on the telephone and in e-mails. Arabic speakers will, depending on the circumstances, go on to exchange semi-ritualized pleasantries perhaps for some time: "How are you?" "How is your health, your family?" The proper Arabic response to these questions is "*Al-Hamdu Lillah*" (this varies slightly with dialects), which may be translated as "Thanks be to God." In other words, conversation, including greetings, is another opportunity for the individual to demonstrate his or her submission to God, as is suitable for a Muslim person. Depending on the situation, there may also be offers of hospitality, tea or coffee, and other refreshments. It is generally polite to accept at least something when it is offered to give the other person the opportunity to demonstrate her or his hospitality and generosity.

In formal written communications or in public addresses, it is customary to begin with the religious invocation that in English is rendered as "In the Name of God the Compassionate, the Merciful." Non-Muslims are not expected to use this form of words and indeed it might be inappropriate to do so. However, the form should be used if the communication is issued by an organization that is owned or largely managed by Muslim people. Visitors are advised either to seek advice from local people in this regard or to pay attention to examples in newspapers, brochures, and so on as to the kind of material and the phrasing required. It should be borne in mind also that it is necessary to be very discreet when using any kind of illustration or graphic together with a communication.

HOSPITALITY

Hospitality is one of the central virtues of Arab society. Its importance derives not just from an innate sense of decency, but from the historical background of life in the desert or on its outskirts. The desert is a harsh environment and, in order for trade and governance to be possible over long distances, it was vital that travelers could be sure that they would receive a safe and hearty welcome when away from home. This has become thoroughly integrated into Emirati society, and all members will take whatever opportunity they can to host other people to whatever might be available. What has changed in recent decades is the amount of money that most people are able to deploy and, hence, the scale of hospitality that many people are now able to offer.

Occasionally it might appear that people are competing with each other to demonstrate their virtue and status by offering ever more lavish refreshments or entertainment. Inevitably, there are occasions when some people will succumb to this kind of competitiveness. Visitors to the UAE should try to steer clear of commenting on this or even appearing to notice, since there is a risk of causing someone to lose status in front of others, and that can be a severe blow to personal pride. Similarly, if enjoying the generosity of one person, it is nearly always a bad idea to comment on generosity or hospitality received elsewhere, especially if the current hospitality appears to be inferior in some way or might be construed to be so. There may be all kinds of familial or long-standing affiliations or rivalries underlying a social episode quite unknown to the visitor.

When accepting an invitation, it is as well to be aware of the length of time you will be expected to attend the event. It may be longer than you imagine, as hosts may anticipate a social occasion lasting for a full day or more (although often much less, of course). You should be prepared to spend this time, or politely make it known that you are able to attend only a portion of the event. Unexpectedly leaving early is likely to be interpreted as an expression of unhappiness or dissatisfaction, and this would reflect poorly on the host's personal sense of hospitality and generosity, as well as affecting other guests' opinions of the same. It may even be seen as a snub. On the other hand, be sensitive to a dropping off of conversation or interaction, especially after a meal is finished, since this may be a signal that it is time to go.

INVITATIONS HOME

Invitations to the home of an Emirati person are quite rare and valuable opportunities to get to know somebody. Being invited to a large compound with an extended family is quite different from being invited to the apartment of a young man alone or a couple. However, even in the latter circumstances it generally represents a show of trust and friendliness. It is appropriate to take a small gift, but don't take anything that might be seen as a slight on the hospitality the host might provide. Don't take food, and especially don't take alcohol. Take something unusual or unexpected, or just ask the person concerned (though you will probably be told that absolutely nothing is required). Remember also that it is normal to take off shoes when entering someone else's house, and be prepared for this. It is also common to sit on cushions or low stools, and this requires some consideration of how to sit. Practice sitting cross-legged, keeping your legs covered and making sure the sole of your foot is not pointing directly at anyone, as this would be insulting.

Depending on the type of social event concerned, there may be a fair amount of sitting down and not doing very much. This may appear unproductive, but it is an important part of getting to know each other and feeling trust in each other's presence. Men and women are likely to be strictly segregated; if men and women jointly visit a house, they will be unlikely to meet inside until it is time for them to leave. Women tend to be busier in crafts and handicrafts and in dressing and beautifying each other than men are, but this varies a great deal. In any case, snacks are likely to be provided as well as one or more meals, and guests urged to take food regularly. It would be impolite to refuse everything so, even if an individual maintains strict dietary habits, it should still be possible to find fruit such as dates or nuts to eat, to show appreciation of generosity. Vegetarianism is not really part of Islamic or

Arabic culture, and meat will be served most of
the time. However, there is also likely to be
available a variety of side dishes, such as bread,
hummus, yogurt, and rice dishes.

MANNERS

It is best always to behave with respect for local
customs, especially religion, and to follow the lead
of Emiratis in the kinds of subjects and issues that
are acceptable to discuss and the ways in which
such discussions should be framed.

In both Arabic and Islamic custom, if not
religion, it is common for the left-hand side of the
body to be considered impure and belonging to
the devil. Consequently, items should be handed
to another person only using the right hand, and
this should also be used to receive items. For
additional emphasis when receiving something
from a person with high status, the left hand may
be placed underneath the right hand or
supporting the wrist, but never in contact with
the hand of the person giving something. Even if
Emirati people occasionally appear to break this
taboo from time to time by grasping a trusted
person with two hands, it is better for the visitor
to be very cautious about doing the same thing as
there are likely to be many factors involved that

are not immediately obvious. In no circumstances should the left hand be used when eating communally, or when taking food from a bowl that other people are also using. Many people prefer to eat with their hands, dipping a piece of bread into a large plate of biryani or taking a piece of meat from a joint. Visitors who are left-handed and naturally wish to use that hand for a variety of functions will need to be especially careful, and might find it helpful to keep that hand in a pocket during such situations. Children are required to write with their right hands irrespective of their natural proclivity and this sometimes hampers them in their educational career. However, this is an area of great cultural significance, and comments about the situation are likely to be considered impolite.

Visitors should also be sensitive to the issues of height and of the feet. It is quite common for people to take off their shoes before visiting a house or a building and certainly in the case of a mosque. Muslim people are also expected to wash their hands and arms up to the elbows and feet and legs up to the knees prior to praying. Anything to do with the feet or with shoes is likely to be considered unclean or impure, and care should be taken not to point the feet at anyone or to expose the soles of the feet carelessly. Further, there is a correlation between status and being highest in the air, even when sitting cross-legged on cushions. Although allowances will be made for visitors, care should also be taken to ensure that the visitor does not tower over people who are seated, or otherwise take a position in which others are looked down upon. Visitors will soon realize when this situation is relevant by observing how other people behave and the posture that they take. Generally being alert and following the examples of others will usually provide enough clues to the right behavior.

Finally, it is necessary to remember that it is considered polite to efface oneself in many social situations—by persuading another person to go through the door first, for example, or by suggesting another person should make a decision involving others, such as in ordering a meal in a restaurant. This, like paying the bill for a group meal, can be a quite intense social struggle. Visitors will most of the time put up a little bit of opposition before giving way gracefully, thereby permitting the other person to gain status by demonstrating generosity of spirit. It is necessary to refuse something several times before convincing another person the item is definitely not wanted. Do not offer an Emirati person something just once and accept the first, ritualized, polite refusal. Make the same offer at least twice more. Remember that Emiratis are Arabs, who prize generosity above almost any other virtue.

chapter five

THE EMIRATIS AT HOME

In line with the example and vision of Sheikh Zayed, the private lives of Emiratis look both to the past and to the future. While many aspects of life may appear intensely conservative to foreign eyes, a more piercing examination will reveal very considerably advanced opinions and lifestyles. Tempting though it is to confuse surface impressions with reality at a deeper level, it is wrong to do so. After all, the young women walking around completely covered by the black *abaya* that covers her entire body and the black *shayla* that covers her head and, in some cases her face as well, might also be using her personal space within her outer clothes to communicate with her friends and family with a hands-free phone and be fully conversant with the latest technology and styles. The *shayla*, meanwhile, appears to be a commonplace square of black silk but is, also, an object of highly designed fashion, albeit that most of the design element is so sophisticated in the pattern and texture that it is impossible to discern unless at very close range. They are designed at some of the best fashion houses of Paris and Milan. Visitors should be wary, in other words, of making superficial judgments.

THE HOUSEHOLD

As wealth has entered the UAE, households, which have traditionally been large, have grown in scope and size, in many if not all cases. It would be expected for a well-established family in most Emirates to live in a large, central house or compound of buildings. Owing to the need to protect women from public view, houses or compounds are customarily surrounded by walls, to stop anyone outside looking in. When people live in apartments or other forms of accommodation, it is also customary for there to be some other means of ensuring privacy. In general terms, unexpected or uninvited guests, whether in person or on the telephone, will be frowned upon by most adults, especially fathers. It is much better to wait for a specific appointment, to enable hosts to make whatever arrangements are deemed necessary.

Most Emirati women have more children than is common in Western countries and this means that households tend to be larger and busier. Consider also that it is normal for an extended family to live in the same establishment. Hence, there might be several generations living together, with their own individual families. Men are entitled to have up to four wives and most will do so in due course, as long as they can afford it. Each of the four wives is required to be treated equally, according to religion and custom. Thus each woman will expect to have her own household within the larger compound and, should one have a new maid or driver, the others must receive the same (although it has rarely been possible for any outsider to determine the extent to which this is actually managed). The relationships between the wives and their various children and relatives can vary considerably. In any case, other family members are likely to be frequent and regular visitors; hence there always seems to be a social occasion.

Since men and women are not generally permitted to occupy the same space, parallel facilities and rooms are built to enable men to have their own dining rooms, seating areas, and bathrooms, and women the same, depending on resources available. For people with less money or less space, social conventions are designed to ensure that women and men can maintain their privacy as required. Children up to the age of seven are generally exempt from this restriction. Girls are

Hand Decorated

For festive occasions, women customarily decorate their hands, and each other's, with henna, a red or orange dye derived from a plant, common in different parts of the Arab world, that has the particular property of adhering to the skin and remaining there. Hands are decorated with all kinds of intricate and often beautiful patterns to mark particular occasions. Constant proximity is also, of course, a means of reinforcing personal relationships.

introduced into segregation on their eighth birthday or thereabouts—bearing in mind that birthdays were not, in the past, traditionally recorded.

GROWING UP IN THE UAE

Growing up in the UAE in the twenty-first century has become quite a pleasurable and privileged thing for the majority of its children. Most children are brought up in large family households in which many playmates are available and where there is enough money to satisfy the demands for consumer goods of various sorts. Of course, there are still many situations to do with family relationships and the presence or absence of parents that can lead to

unhappiness but, on the whole, these seem to occur less frequently than in most other countries. Until the age of eight boys and girls mix with and play with each other, but after that age girls become sequestered in different parts of the house to an extent dependent on the particular views of the heads of the household and the practical details of the layout of the house or compound. Since most men will wish to marry up to the permitted maximum of four wives, this leads to a variety of different parenting styles, as women are brought to the UAE from other countries—nearly always from other Islamic societies. Incoming women and their family members who may accompany them will bring their own customs and tastes, which lend some variety to the ways in which children are raised.

Schools are generally well resourced, and if they have a fault it is that teachers customarily must rely for their livelihood on not upsetting the students, some of whom, of course, learn to play on this. School vacations can be a little restricted, especially for girls, but family vacations overseas are common, and this leads to a broadening of experience. There is also likely to be easy access to entertainment via modern media, television, and the Internet, although content is routinely vetted to ensure that it is appropriate.

Until recently, education in the UAE has been dominated by the rote learning approach, in which students learn by heart what teachers prescribe for them and then are rewarded for repeating it verbatim. Teachers were considered to be people of good status and their word was not to be challenged. This has changed somewhat in recent years as more liberal approaches to education have been introduced. However, teachers are still generally respected in society.

FAMILY OCCASIONS

With the large size of most families and households, there are family occasions on a pretty regular basis. This is, of course, a good thing, in that it offers many opportunities for families to celebrate with each other and to reaffirm relationships through feasting, giving gifts, and generally being together, although men and women will do so separately. It also provides people with the opportunity to learn how to share the limelight with others, as a single birthday, for example, is not likely to stand out so much from the welter of other occasions. The same also necessarily applies to sadder occasions, such as funerals, where mourners are also likely to have to share the occasion with others.

Family occasions will generally be held in the house, since in that way both men and women can participate in their separate areas. However, it is also increasingly common for young men to wish to celebrate their own occasions in public, favoring restaurants and clubs, according to taste. Gatherings at home tend to center on the communal meal, since this is a traditional method of celebration. There may also be singing and ululating in the women's section, and perhaps poetry recitations or singing among the men.

The modern world has impacted upon family occasions in the UAE as much as it has in other countries and societies. Young people in particular may prefer to be in contact with their friends through their cell phones or to engage in online chat or games rather than spend time with their many relatives. Negotiation and compromise are the order of the day in UAE households as much as they are elsewhere.

DAILY LIFE

Daily life for people in the UAE varies enormously depending on who is involved and what is the occasion. For all people, the daily routine is very likely to be punctuated by the five daily calls to prayer and also by any social or cultural obligations. Men are much more likely than women to work outside the house or to be able to go out in public without various precautions. A great deal of the daily routine is carried out at something of a distance from the outside world, since it involves moving from air-conditioned homes or offices by similarly cooled cars to other houses or offices. It is quite possible for people to dress for a much cooler climate than that of the UAE because they spend their whole time in an artificial environment.

In the past, women's domestic work would have involved trips to the various *souks*, together with food preparation and housework. Much of this has been eased by labor-saving devices or through hiring domestic help from overseas. Senior women may wish to supervise domestic arrangements so that they comply with their own particular standards but, in many cases, there is little real need

for this. However, overseeing a large household and the numerous logistical tasks this requires can actually provide quite substantial levels of practical experience in management. These skills are in some cases allowed to

flourish outside the home, since it is possible for women to manage organizations of various types without coming into inappropriate physical proximity to a man to whom she is not married. Women who work usually take positions in the civil service, although some run their own businesses, including schools and clinics or hospitals.

Women may also be able to manage their affairs through an online presence, and people are still  exploring the ways in which UAE women may come into contact with the rest of the world through the mediation of the screen and keyboard. At the very least, using the Internet permits women a much wider and more rewarding shopping experience. However, it is likely that online social networking and similar issues will become much more important in due course. For example, Emirati people are as keen as everyone else to participate in Facebook, YouTube, or similar networking sites, although this of course raises many issues of propriety that are still emerging.

The telecommunications infrastructure that supports the Internet in the UAE is strong and stable, and people feel confident about their ability to go online to operate their businesses and affairs, although there are other difficulties attached to living in the country in this respect.

BOYS AND GIRLS

As we have seen, the lives of boys and girls differ significantly for religious reasons. This takes a physical form in the different clothes that each is expected to wear, as well as the roles that each should play in the family and in society. In recent years, thanks in part to the example of Sheikh Zayed, it has become much more usual for girls to be educated up to and including the college level. The range of topics that they are permitted to study has also expanded somewhat, with exceptions, although the head of the household is always expected to wield a veto in the case of debate. However, as in most countries, parents do not always hear about everything that their children discuss at school or university.

Childhood in the UAE is also a strongly religious experience, since the Muslim religion suffuses every aspect of daily life. This ranges from daily study and learning of the Koran as well as observation of the five daily calls to prayer and putting into practice, as much as children can, the other Pillars of Islam. Even if it were the case that a parent's devotion to religion might be less than enthusiastic, that parent will still take pains to ensure that children are brought up to be as good Muslims as they possibly can be, and to appear so in public.

chapter six

TIME OUT

Cultures with harsh climates often have extensive periods of leisure during the day, since it has been difficult or unhealthy to work throughout the length of the day. These hours are customarily spent with people of the same gender and this has had an impact upon shaping the kinds of activity that take place. Much time is spent relaxing and talking, without appearing to do very much but in reality constantly creating and confirming personal and familial network relationships. In the modern world, new forms of technology have greatly broadened the kinds of leisure activity that Emiratis may choose to pursue, but cultural conditions remain important. People prefer to do things in the company of a group of their family members and friends. Being alone or wanting to be alone is not a strong part of Emirati culture.

SHOPPING FOR PLEASURE

There is a great deal of retail space in the UAE—probably rather more than sustained demand really justifies—and a number of the high-value brand-name shops seem to have opened stores for status rather than

commercial purposes. However, this does mean that people who enjoy shopping or who, in fact, just need to buy something, usually have a wide choice of places to visit. As ever, Abu Dhabi and Dubai are the best locations for this. Shopping centers may be themed in some way or else be the scene for expensive lotteries and giveaways. All large

centers are cleaned regularly and have their own security, so they may be considered safe for families.

More traditional means of shopping are provided in the *souks*, the covered markets, which, given the heat, are best visited during the evening and, consequently, are usually only open then anyway. *Souks* have stalls that sell all manner of goods, from locally or regionally produced textiles, electronic goods, crockery, kitchen goods, and spices and herbs. Arabic textiles and perfumes can make a distinctive gift, and there are also various UAE-themed gifts, such as camels, wooden statues, and the like. Few of these items are actually made in the UAE. Most of the manufactured goods in the country are not of export quality. For an authentic gift from the UAE, it is probably necessary to buy dates, or locally made

chocolates, or candies made in regional or Lebanese styles that are very nicely presented and also delicious. Most confectionery items are high in calories and will not suit every diet. Food, in general, is designed for taste rather than nutrition, although steps in health education are being taken. Still, it is likely to take some years before these become embedded into the fabric of domestic life.

CULTURAL ACTIVITIES

It is common for people to ignore the cultural attractions that are on their doorstep and prefer to visit and think about those that are far away. This is as true of the UAE as it is of most other countries. Consequently, it is usually only as schoolchildren that Emiratis visit and enjoy the cultural treasures of their country—those that are available to the public's scrutiny, that is. Many important cultural artifacts are kept as part of private households and may be appreciated, therefore, at any time by their owners and guests. This means that the public areas tend to be chiefly the preserve of visitors and tourists.

Museums

Museums with interesting collections of historical artifacts from the UAE and from cultures that traded with it in the past include those at Al Ain, Ras al-Kheimah, Sharjah, and Dubai. The Dubai Museum is located in the Al Fahidi Fort, which is itself a sight worth seeing. Sharjah has several linked museums, including the Archaeological Museum, the Heritage Museum, the Science Museum, the Islamic Museum, and the Natural History Museum and Desert Park. This last-named is popular with

children, owing in part to its Children's Zoo and Arabian Endangered Animals Breeding Center. The museums take a modern approach to science that is somewhat at odds with the worldview of the more conservative religious thinkers, which makes an interesting contrast. The Heritage Museum consists of several sites, including forts, a house restored to the décor and style of the past, and an old but restored *souk*. Most such cultural attractions designate a day, or part of a day, for women and children only, charge low or no entrance fees, and open reduced hours on Friday. Check ahead for hours of operation, as there is one day a week, often Monday, when attractions are closed. Most institutions have their own Web site; otherwise information can be found in one of the general UAE compendium sites.

The "Desert Experience"

There are various activities laid out for tourists to give them a taste of the life of the country. Some tour operators organize a trip into the desert to a camp where dinner is served and music is played, perhaps with a non-Emirati belly dancer in attendance as well. Such tourist activities are only tangentially related to the reality of the UAE's past, but can still be enjoyable for all that. Thoughtful visitors might wonder whether the "touristification" of cultural activities demeans the local people and their culture, as has happened in some other countries. This has mostly not happened in the UAE because of certain restrictions placed on tour operators. However, that does not mean that it will never happen.

Performance

Most Emirates have established one or more
cultural foundations that put on appropriate and
genuine re-creations of the past and its expression,
often focusing on the spoken word accompanied
by music or dance. Visitors should check ahead for
forthcoming events and performances, as well as
inquiring whether they are intended for any
audience. Some performances are for men only
and some are for women only.

EATING OUT

The UAE has a range of eating establishments to
suit every budget and taste, including
representatives of all the best cuisines of the world.
Restaurants include five-star hotel-based
operations in the larger cities, which can be very
expensive, especially when it is the case that
substantial amounts of fresh ingredients must be
flown into the country on a daily basis. Large
hotels of this sort are organized and staffed
customarily to the highest international standards.
Some of them offer all-you-can-eat international
buffets for comparatively low costs.

Other restaurants include American fast-food
and upscale establishments, which are often the
best place for family dining. There are also

restaurants aimed at providing specific low-cost cuisines to particular ethnic communities and migrant workers; these can be quite basic eateries where only men are anticipated to be customers. Women and children are, of course, generally welcomed in restaurants throughout the country, but they may find the environment uncomfortable in these more modest places. It is common for fast-food restaurants and some food court outlets not to provide cutlery, as people are content to eat with their fingers.

The more expensive restaurants have a special dispensation to sell alcohol. Most restaurants do not sell alcohol, especially those that are not part of hotels or designated tourist areas. Many restaurants are prepared to deliver to customers' homes, given that their premises may not be set up for family dining. The service is generally reliable and there is rarely any additional cost levied, given the cheapness of oil and labor costs. It is also possible to hire cooks and serving staff to come to a house or business to provide food for a specific occasion.

TABLE MANNERS

Emirati hosts are, perhaps to a fault, generous and solicitous that guests eat fully and with enjoyment. This tends to lead to an expectation that a large amount of food will be eaten with relish. Visitors are advised to go without the meal before if they anticipate being placed in this situation. In the past, guests would belch to demonstrate they are replete, and some still continue with this practice, although it is no longer widely expected from foreigners. Remember that the left hand is considered unclean and should be used as little as possible, especially when communal dishes are offered, which is quite frequently the case.

In addition to feasting hard and long, guests should also be prepared to be fulsome and apparently genuine in praise of and gratitude to the host, who will accept compliments gracefully. Meals are customarily followed by Arabic coffee, which can be quite strong, as well as cigarettes in many cases. The shared meal is generally considered to be the centerpiece of an act of hospitality, and a lull after it is finished is often a sign that it is the right time to make excuses and leave.

COFFEE-SHOP CULTURE

All across the Middle East and the Eastern Mediterranean, men gather together to discuss the day's events, politics, and life in general with their fellows. Customarily the place they will gather will be a coffeehouse of some sort. Tea, coffee, or various other types of soft drink are available, perhaps with some snacks or sweets. Newspapers may be provided, as well as hookah pipes for those who enjoy smoking—and traditionally most men involved do enjoy smoking. In addition to talking and smoking, men might also enjoy playing chess or a local game. Women are not, customarily, banned from entering these places, but their presence usually makes everyone feel a little uncomfortable. This type of culture is prevalent in the UAE, with the difference that many of the more traditional coffee shops have been superseded by luxurious, air-conditioned outlets in shopping centers or hotels.

Hubbly-Bubbly

Emirati leisure time tends to extend until quite late at night, especially during Ramadan or other public holidays. One means of relaxing is to hang out in a luxurious café and smoke hookah pipes. These "hubbly-bubbly" water pipes are both picturesque and fragrant, and people who enjoy smoking cigarettes are likely to enjoy this experience too.

These modern places are more likely to be family- and female-friendly than the more traditional types, which often have the further disadvantage of being quite warm.

Nonsmokers might like to note that smoking is permitted in rather a wider range of establishments than is now common in most Western countries. There is not much that can be done about this, other than searching for places that have nonsmoking areas. People who cannot tolerate the smoke will have to stay away from these public places.

NIGHTCLUBS AND BARS

Nightclubs have become popular in Dubai, and attract a considerable amount of international attention, including cross-border visitors, in addition to the celebrities and high-profile athletes from the West who have made Dubai one of the most fashionable places to visit. The behavior of men in particular in nightclubs differs from the normal run of manners in Emirati society and it is better to avoid those whose inexperience of this form of leisure makes them likely to cause a scene.

The laws of supply and demand apply in the UAE as they do in just about every country in the world and, consequently, illicit appetites may also be satisfied. The UAE police treat illegal or what may be termed sinful behavior quite severely and visitors are best advised to stay away from any of the very few establishments that seem to have a dubious reputation.

SPORTS

Sports in the UAE very often means football (soccer), with Emiratis following a wide range of usually the larger and better-known European club teams. English, Italian, and Spanish football leagues are all followed with great interest. However, the UAE also has its own domestic league, which is keenly contested and of quite a high level. Now that the Asian Football Association has organized club-level competitions, bringing together the best of the continent's club teams, this has added new intensity to domestic games that act as a gateway to the larger and more prestigious

competitions. The executives of local teams are generally quite generous in offering salaries and bonuses to players and so can attract international stars to supplement the efforts of the local players.

The UAE has also emerged as a major sponsor of soccer, with Emirates Airlines acting as sponsor of Arsenal FC, with its new stadium named the Emirates Stadium. The company previously sponsored Chelsea. Multimillion dollar deals have also been completed with the world governing body FIFA and the French club Paris St. Germain, among others.

However, there is much more to sports in the UAE than just football. World-class speedboat racing makes for a spectacular watching experience, as too do the motor racing events and the camel racing. In 2005, the UAE government introduced strict new regulations aimed at protecting the camel jockeys after repeated allegations of child labor and human trafficking. Subsequently, more than a thousand young people who had been part of the camel racing world have been repatriated, mostly to South Asia. A rehabilitation and recovery center was also established for those who had fallen foul of unscrupulous operators. Visitors can now enjoy the camel racing with an easy conscience in terms of the treatment of the jockeys—they have been replaced by robo-jockeys. These mechanical devices are perched on the backs of the camels and communication between the camel owner and robo-jockeys takes place by radio, which enables some control over the racing tactics of the camel involved. This is similar to operating a radio-controlled car, but the robo-jockey manipulates the camel's reins and causes it to change course and go faster or slow down.

Other sports that are supported in the UAE include sailing, including dhow sailing, motor sports organized in the desert, and, largely for the benefit of expatriate workers, international cricket and rugby events. Water sports, martial arts, and aerobatics are other activities that can be watched from time to time, while leading tennis players regularly appear in the high-profile and well-rewarded competitions. Since UAE sports bodies are able to provide high-quality facilities together with large cash and gift payments for performance, leading international competitors in a range of sports are more than willing to compete there in various events. However, the sports authorities take steps to ensure the rise in standards of local athletes, and foreign imports into the local football league have had only limited success.

OUT OF TOWN

The areas of the UAE away from the urban centers may appear, to the outsider, to be unpopulated and rather featureless spaces. However, for the Emiratis, these are the places that saw the origins of their people, and where

their long and distinguished history has been enacted. Visitors who want to explore the rural areas will learn a great deal more if they have a knowledgeable guide or advisor. Another perspective may be gained if the guide is knowledgeable about the flora and fauna of the desert. It is something of a cliché to observe that the desert is full of life, contrary to expectations, but you'll need the company of an expert to gain a full appreciation of this fact.

Others might enjoy moonlit picnics and the romance of the night sky, which, away from the bright city lights, can be exceptionally clear in the desert and enable the viewer to see shooting stars (meteors), planets, and satellites that are normally impossible to see.

Wildlife

Those with an interest in the local flora and fauna will also enjoy a trip into the desert to observe what there is to be seen. Birds are particularly plentiful in the skies over the UAE, with perhaps the most striking being the birds of prey, including eagles, falcons, buzzards, and owls. Closer to the sea are terns, ospreys, and occasional flamingos. On the ground are wild goats and camels, the rare Arabian leopard, hedgehogs, jackals, and wolves. However, animals tend to be cautious and are rarely seen unless special care is taken by observers to be discreet. Most plants to be found these days are the results of the government's various greenery projects. Nevertheless, it is possible to see the dwarf mangrove plants near the salty swamplands and the plants that bloom after the occasional rain.

Dune-Bashing

One of the most popular forms of entertainment amongst adventurous souls in the UAE is to take their four-wheel drive vehicles into the desert and chase up and down the sand dunes. The dunes can be several tens of meters tall and steep enough to prove a challenge to the engine and driving skills of most vehicles. Many enjoy risking their vehicle against the force of gravity, and like to find out quite how acute an angle their cars can manage, without toppling over into the soft sand.

A Warning

The desert can be an alluring place, but it is also a dangerous one, owing to the heat and the dangers of dehydration and disorientation. Visitors should always take precautions before setting off into the desert, including making sure that they have plenty of water and some emergency provisions on board their vehicle, which should itself be properly checked. The travel plans and itinerary should always be left with a reliable person who can alert the necessary authorities should the travelers fail to return according to schedule. It is also prudent to check with the government as to when and where military exercises may be planned.

chapter seven

TRAVEL, HEALTH, & SAFETY

ROADS AND TRAFFIC

The presence of oil and gas and their cheapness for motorists have contributed toward a culture in which personal mobility is greatly valued. This culture is supported by more deep-rooted factors, including the remote, isolated, desert origin of many tribes and the desire to have women protected from public view. The consequence is that people drive everywhere. Large and expensive cars are very much favored, both to accommodate large numbers of family members and also for reasons of status and prestige.

Most cars and other vehicles have tinted windows. There are practical reasons for this, including the very strong sunlight, which can make traveling by car uncomfortable, and also the wish, in the case of women, not to be seen. There is a careful balance to be negotiated

between the desire of people not to be seen and the desire of the police and other authorities to be able to see who is inside a vehicle and whether such people might be doing something (or just being somewhere) that would be of interest to the police. The result is that the degree of tinting permissible depends on who owns the vehicle and who is expected to travel within it. A vehicle that is customarily used to transport Emirati women will be permitted to have more deeply tinted windows than one used for anyone else. It is often possible to tell how important a car's passengers are by how difficult it is to make out if there is anyone inside at all.

Large vehicles are expected to restrict themselves to the inside lane and not to pass any others. This regulation is policed quite strongly, and professional drivers are reluctant to take actions that could have a negative impact on their job and evaluation. This can cause some delays when a phalanx of large, slow-moving vehicles blocks the progress of large but otherwise faster-moving vehicles. Patience is a virtue.

Local Transportation
In most Emirates, it is not difficult to find a taxi to take a passenger wherever is required. These are

comparatively cheap in Abu Dhabi, and rather more expensive in Dubai and elsewhere. There are also numerous small minibus services for transport within an Emirate or from one to another. These are mostly used by comparatively low-paid

workers, and women and children may find them slightly uncomfortable. In Dubai, in particular, ferries are important in transferring people across the Creek, which separates the *souks* from most of the residential and hotel areas. These are cheap, frequent, and a fun way to cross the water.

Owing to the low price of gas and the generally generous salaries, the majority of people or families have a vehicle to transport themselves from place to place. In truth, some of the richer families have a fleet of vehicles to meet their various needs. Traffic is mostly light throughout the country, apart perhaps from the busiest times of day in Dubai and Sharjah and when crowds have gathered for a special occasion. The roads linking the major cities and Emirates are generally of a high standard, and dangers occur mostly when people drive recklessly. Road traffic accident statistics reveal proportionately more fatalities in the UAE than for other countries at a comparable level of development. Don't drink and drive—there is zero tolerance, and imprisonment and corporal punishment (whipping) may result.

It is not difficult to obtain a driver's license. You have to have an eye test, and to give a small blood sample, which is used for recording your blood group in the event of emergency after a road traffic accident. Certain hospitals are designated for both these purposes. Forms for completion are in Arabic, and non-Arabic speakers will need help to complete them. For medical and emergency services dial 999.

Purchasing a vehicle requires a residence visa, which all long-term visitors will have in any case. Owing to the high level of people entering and leaving the country after completing contracts, there are healthy secondhand car markets in addition to attractive prices for new vehicles. Very few people use motorcycles, owing to the heat and the dangers they pose. Those drivers who go "dune-bashing" (see page 118) buy or rent a 4 x 4 or sports utility vehicle. Rental prices are generally reasonable for a range of vehicles.

It is also not uncommon for people to buy or use quite sophisticated vehicles such as speedboats, yachts, jet skis, and other water sports utilities. People who enjoy large and powerful vehicles of all types will find much to entertain them in the UAE.

Intercity Travel

People traveling from place to place in the UAE are generally polite and friendly, although they will expect that family proprieties will be observed if women are in the party. Few Emiratis travel by public transportation, although in the outlying areas this is more common for the poorer citizens.

Public transportation vehicles take advantage of the generally well-appointed roads. The well-heeled might think nothing of hiring a taxi for a two-hour trip, but there are suitable alternatives. Coach and bus services link the major cities and offer a reasonable degree of comfort, without being too  expensive. Since there is comparatively little traffic, they are usually punctual. Minivans provide links with intercity services terminating at bus stations outside the city centers. Most stations are themselves comparatively well appointed, clean, and safe, as are nearly all the public spaces in the UAE. Buses provide separate sections for women and children, and are air-conditioned, although accommodation is a little more crowded in minivans.

Rumors of large-scale mass transportation systems involving railways or ferries persist, but these have yet to materialize, perhaps because of lack of sustained demand. However, as the county's importance as an import and reexport center continues to increase, so the need for better transportation links with neighboring Emirates and states will also escalate. The UAE now has admirable air transportation links with cities around the world, and already has three international airports.

WHERE TO STAY

There is a wide range of accommodation available in the UAE, with a great deal of emphasis placed upon the five-star hotels and luxury establishments. These include the famous Burj El-Arab, which is working on gaining its seventh star, and many other hotels of international high standard, primarily in the three most developed Emirates of

Abu Dhabi, Dubai, and Sharjah. These hotels can usually be booked online and, given the large number of rooms available, will periodically offer very good deals in off-peak times. Hotels may also be willing to handle visa applications, which can be convenient when inviting overseas guests.

Burj El-Arab

The world's most luxurious and, by common consent, best hotel is located on the coastline of Dubai, and its shape of a giant, billowing sail towering into the sky has become a modern icon for the country. The Burj El-Arab offers more facilities than anyone could ever expect, including underwater restaurants reached by private submarine. The price of staying there, of course, reflects its luxury and quality.

Most hotels will offer buffet lunches and dinners, as well as international breakfast. Guests can anticipate that these will be *halal* meals based on the Arabic style. Rooms are nearly always clean and pleasant.

In addition to upscale accommodation, there is also a range of lower-cost accommodation aimed primarily at the less-skilled or less well-

paid migrant workers. These are generally
decent enough, although not always convenient
for women and children.

Large numbers of apartments are available for
visitors, mostly organized so that migrant
communities can live in close proximity to each
other. These can offer very large amounts of space
internally—the kind of accommodation that is
perhaps more familiar to Americans than
Europeans. It is customary for employers to
organize this, and to make block bookings
according to need. However, it is possible to
manage a move to another location if desired. Most
apartments are provided empty, and visitors will be
issued with an allowance for furnishing them. This
helps to explain the enormous number of furniture

and furnishings shops that are available across the country. There is little "do it yourself," and installation services are usually provided by retailers as a matter of course, as well as delivery. However, efficiency in this sector does tend to vary.

It is also possible to rent tents and live at least temporarily in the desert. However, this is not recommended to anyone who does not have the requisite skills or indeed permissions.

HEALTH

In a society with such modern infrastructure as the UAE, it is not surprising that some of the very best and most professional hospitals are to be found. However, many of these hospitals are comparatively small and also rather expensive, since nearly all component parts and staff must be imported. Consequently, many people with unusual or specific health problems now travel overseas to destinations such as India, Singapore, or Thailand, in order to take advantage of lower-cost health care. For migrant workers, of course, much health care beyond the very basic will be out of their price range, and either second-rate care is sought or the worker will seek to return to the home country or some other, cheaper, location for a short period. To cover the costs of health care, employers are expected to offer a comprehensive health insurance scheme. However, the constantly rising costs of health care, especially given the wider range of conditions that can now be treated, mean that such schemes can scarcely ever be really comprehensive. Further, health problems that may have been brought about by what are considered in the country to be sinful activities are unlikely to be covered by insurance. Salaries being offered to expatriate workers in the UAE are generally declining and the amount that individuals are expected to contribute to their health insurance from those salaries is increasing.

It may be noted that all migrants wishing to be employed in the UAE must be tested for the presence of HIV/AIDS, and permission to remain will be refused if the virus is found. It is claimed that there is no incidence of HIV/AIDS in the country.

The high standard of living for most of Emirati society has meant that standards of health have also improved. Few of the conventional treatable diseases or conditions remain, but people are now starting to suffer from the problems brought about by affluence, including obesity leading to heart disease and diabetes, especially mature-onset diabetes. Statistics show that more than half of all deaths in the country may be attributed to cardiovascular disease, road traffic accidents, cancer, and congenital abnormalities. In the last-named case, blood abnormalities such as thalassemia are particularly prevalent in the UAE because of the high incidence of intermarriage within a comparatively small stock of people.

Each Emirate operates its own health care system, generally slanted toward specific local issues. Research is conducted at certain high-technology facilities. However, it is not considered suitable for Emirati women to enter into medicine as a profession because it would expose them to the physical bodies of men to whom they were not married and, indeed, even the study of medicine is impaired because textbooks will be excised of any pictures or illustrations that are considered inappropriate for women to view.

SAFETY

The UAE is a generally safe country. The rule of law is strongly enforced, although there may be some preferential treatment in certain cases.

Fear of detection and capture, together with lack of motivation, keeps acts of theft and violence at a comparatively low rate. Since crime is strongly linked to poverty and inequality, no foreigners are permitted to live in the country if they do not have steady, gainful employment. This is different in the corporate world, to some extent, in that the temptations for some managers to defraud companies or customers may become great. However, low levels of crime are not the same as zero levels, particularly in the big city of Dubai, where the temptations are greatest.

Perhaps the most dangerous thing to do in the UAE is to drive along the roads, especially the excellent highways that link the main urban areas. These highways are so well maintained that they seem to encourage people to drive faster than they really should, and at high speeds even a momentary loss of control is sufficient to lead to fatalities, as frequently occurs in the country. Some police patrols and automatic radar systems have been introduced to try to reduce the incidence of road traffic accidents, but these do not represent serious deterrents to many people.

Single women may be harassed if they travel alone, especially if they are dressed in a way that attracts attention. Given that Emirati women, even when permitted to travel in a public space, are completely covered by *abaya* and *shayla*, any other form of dress tends to stand out from the crowd. This can inspire some men to make derogatory comments and pay unwanted attention. This attention can be deflected by traveling with a "chaperone," or by dressing in the way that Middle Eastern women do. Avoid dressing exactly like an Emirati, because it is illegal for a foreigner to pretend to be an Emirati citizen with a view to obtaining preferential treatment. However, police are reluctant to approach women, no matter who they are.

There are grounds for believing that abuse of domestic servants and of certain employees takes place in some Emirati households and organizations. However, visitors are unlikely to come across these issues. People moving to the UAE for work should be aware that labor unions are not recognized and there is very little opportunity for any appeal against any decision reached by an employer. In general terms, if a contract is canceled for any reason, the former employee may be expected to leave the country together with any dependents and possessions within forty-eight hours. It is better to avoid such a situation and to manage relationships with important employers and representatives prudently.

The police themselves, like the lower ranks of the military, are mostly recruited from other Middle Eastern countries. They have strict orders to uphold the law as it is given to them, and so rarely show discretion. Be polite when dealing with them, and follow their instructions scrupulously. Seek their assistance only when really necessary.

chapter eight

BUSINESS BRIEFING

THE BUSINESS LANDSCAPE

The United Arab Emirates is one of the pools of calmness and rapid but stable development arranged along the coast of the Persian Gulf, which flourish despite the often chaotic conditions in its neighbors across the water. Although no one can predict the future with accuracy, it seems likely that the UAE will be able to continue on its present course in the future. Investors can have as much confidence putting funds into the country as they can in any other country in the world. The range of industries and economic sectors in which investment is

possible is also increasing greatly, as the UAE's leaders prepare a diversified economy in anticipation of the inevitable depletion of oil reserves at some stage in the future.

BUSINESS CULTURE

How business is done in the UAE depends to
a significant extent on the business partner.
Sometimes it is not easy to tell who is the real
boss. Nearly all locally incorporated companies
are registered to Emirati citizens, but not all
owners are interested in their businesses. In
some extreme cases, they will not even be aware
that the business has been registered in their
name. In other cases, they expect to be able to
make all the important decisions and have
appointed general managers with a view to
having all relevant information brought to them
for the decision to be made. The consequences
of this for the visitor are that, first of all, it is
necessary to be patient and tolerant and, second,
it is very helpful to do what research is necessary
to find out who exactly is in charge.

If the people you are dealing with change,
the business culture involved in a particular
transaction will also necessarily change.
However, the physical spaces in which business
deals take place tend to be similar: large,
spacious offices with excellent, even luxurious,
facilities. These surroundings usually mean that
proceedings have a certain additional feeling of
formality, and that adds time. Visitors should
factor in some additional time for such

meetings while reflecting that the excellent traffic management systems enable most of that time to be regained somewhere along the line.

BUSINESS ETHICS

Emiratis are as honest and hardworking as the people of any other country, but they are also subject to the same temptations. Since many deals involve large payments not always made in a fully transparent way, it is not surprising that there are occasions when some people fail to adhere to the highest possible levels of behavior. However, since the country relies to a great extent upon its reputation for good and honest dealing, serious efforts are spent to ensure that any misdemeanors are rapidly tracked down and any misappropriated funds restored to their rightful owners. The international ethics rating organization Transparency International ranked the UAE the fourteenth-most corruption free country in the world in 2006, just behind Singapore and Spain, and ahead of countries such as France, Israel, and Hong Kong.

This does not mean that there is never any fraud or corruption, of course. The sheer amount of money involved in some deals and attached to industries such as oil and banking can represent very real temptations to the managers and executives involved. While people can be perfectly honest in the course of everyday life, the sudden prospect of obtaining perhaps millions of dollars can change a person's behavior altogether and make otherwise ruinous risks appear worthwhile.

In modern business, companies are expected to demonstrate their ethical commitment in terms of their impact on their stakeholders (other groups of people who rely upon the firm in one way or another) and in their impact on society and on the environment. In common with those of many other countries, UAE firms are only beginning to come to grips with their environmental impact, and the oil companies, of course, have a very different perspective from that of most other people. Emirati laws that prevent freedom of association for trades unionists and the lack of collective bargaining rights will be considered unethical by many people.

BUSINESS ETIQUETTE

It is advisable to have business cards ready to hand out when meeting new people, and to remember to offer one with the right hand. To show deference, you can receive a card from someone else with both hands, but this is not compulsory, as it would be in Japan or Korea. Expect to be offered coffee or tea at the start of any meeting, and accept at least one cup. Doing otherwise would be considered rude, although taking more than one sip is not necessary. Cups are small, in the Arabic style. When refusing another cup, gently waggle the cup between thumb and forefinger to indicate you have had enough. Wait calmly for the meeting to turn to the issues you are interested in discussing, but be ready to address them when the opportunity comes.

Face and status issues are important in business as well as in social situations. Permit the senior person in any situation to take the leading role and enjoy the privileges of being host. This will not generally impact upon the nature of any important discussion, but it is usually important to ensure that dignity is retained by all those who have it to maintain. In general, it costs little in time or effort in real terms to allow people to settle themselves into such ways that they can deal with their own status issues before moving on to the next stage of business.

Many businesspeople will maintain one or more business or technical advisors for reasons that are not transparent to other potential business partners. Advisors should be accorded respect and tolerance to the extent that the status of the advised person dictates. On some occasions, advisors may come and go during meetings so as to complete various confidential assignments and commissions of their own. This, like the answering of cell phones during an address, should not be construed as a lack of respect, but simply the way of doing things. Further, the moment at which a decision is actually made may not be entirely obvious. On some occasions, a consensus will emerge from discussions and in others a moment comes when eye contact between significant decision makers will be sufficient to determine success or failure. Visitors who might be expecting a lengthy period of due process or similar checking may occasionally find themselves flummoxed by what happens on these occasions. On other occasions, of course, business deals are entirely standardized according to the Western model.

Note also that it is possible for there to be struggles, often tacit, between two or more people as to who should be recognized as the senior in any situation. Unlike in many East Asian societies, this cannot normally be resolved by simply working out who was born first, but instead involves determination of familial and tribal ties and other details not obvious to the outsider. Visitors should in general terms avoid becoming involved in these situations and allow those concerned to resolve it according to their own cultural practices.

PRESENTATIONS

Although a great deal of business practice in the UAE has come to resemble international best practice, it is advisable nevertheless to be prudent about the use of visual symbols and to be sensitive to the views and beliefs of other people. In the first place, it should be borne in mind that in general Islamic thought it is considered inappropriate by many to portray people in any way, and, in some cases, animals or anthropomorphic versions of inanimate objects can also be a cause for offense. It is best to avoid illustrations that are not wholly abstract. Indeed, any graphic or suggestion of men and women appearing in the same physical space should be eliminated. Similarly, sound effects and sound files should also be

considered carefully for possible causes of misunderstanding. It is also necessary to be careful with portrayals of people from the UAE or its neighbors, any use of Arabic writing, and religious iconography. The likelihood of causing offense, presumably without intent, is such that it is much more sensible to be safe than to be sorry.

NEGOTIATIONS

The ways in which negotiations take place in the UAE vary considerably, depending on the industry, the knowledge, and the experience of the people involved, especially in terms of any international experience. Traditional forms of negotiation depend to a considerable extent upon finding common ties and affiliations as a means of assessing trustworthiness, after which the business details can be dealt with. Expect, therefore, to spend some time while partners work out who is related to whom and what other connections exist. UAE business executives with international experience are likelier to get down to business more promptly and follow a negotiation style closer to Western versions.

Most Emirati managers are used to dealing with other people, and to occupying a position in which people come to them with propositions of various sorts. Consequently, they are quite happy to reject deals that do not appeal to them and expect proposals to be structured in ways they might consider attractive. This means that negotiations can become quite tough.

CONTRACTS

Contracts are created in line with standard international best practice. Once a contract is signed, the parties involved will be expected to adhere strictly to its provisions. In traditional Arabic culture, a contract would not really be considered necessary, since it is the underlying relationship between the different people involved that provides the guarantee of compliance with any agreement. Indeed, there may be occasions on which this old-fashioned approach to business may be carried out between people who know and trust each other sufficiently. However, experience of dealing with international business partners and the need for transparency in deals has persuaded most UAE businesspeople of the value of contracts and adhering to them.

UAE law is used to regulate contracts, and this is determined by a judge working alone or as part of a panel of three when court proceedings are required. Anticipate that contracts and documentation will be in Arabic, even when business partners speak good English. All documents for dealing with the government will be in Arabic. It is wise to ask for advice at the relevant Embassy or Chamber of Commerce as to recommended translation agencies, and establish a working relationship with one.

MEETINGS

Meetings are a very important part of UAE business culture; indeed, sometimes it can seem that holding a meeting is an end in its own right and need not have any particular purpose other than getting people together. Of course, this very much depends on the individuals concerned, the importance attached to the business involved, and the pressure of circumstances. However, it is generally the case that initial meetings must be held at the start of any new business venture so that people can get to know each other, and start to feel comfortable in each other's presence and with the idea of doing business together. These initial meetings are almost entirely social in nature, since they involve the serving of tea and coffee and refreshments, together with general conversation. In the past, this process could continue for some hours before any hint of business could be brought into play and, in some cases, more than one such meeting would need to be held before the commercial aspect could be initiated. These days, this process is generally much abridged, since people are busier and also have much more international and cross-cultural experience than before. Besides which, there are so many more business opportunities now than there were in the past. Consequently, the process of mutual acclimatization has been much reduced. Even so, the niceties of entertainment and hospitality are still likely to be observed scrupulously.

Historically, when a person wished to meet an important social or commercial figure, that person would go to the appropriate tent and wait. The amount of time that would pass before the petitioner was admitted to the presence depended on the relative status of those involved. However, the petitioner would be admitted sooner or later. It would not be practical to operate such a system in the modern world but some aspects of this practice do still linger. For example, there is the belief that everyone will get access to the leader if they are sufficiently persistent, and there is an obligation on the shoulders of the leader to be available to employees. Foreign-born businessmen who hold managerial or executive positions in the UAE should probably consider the implications of this historical background for their own position. Perhaps it would be possible for the manager to permit access to all those people who may wish to consult him or her, at least on specific occasions?

Anticipate also that other people may come in and out of the meeting room on unrelated business. This is common, and the visitor should simply pause if necessary to allow other conversations to take place. Don't address newly arriving people without being invited to do so by others in the meeting, and avoid showing any irritation or impatience with interruptions. On the other hand, do set main objectives for a meeting and focus on these as much as possible, no matter how sidetracked the discussion might become.

DEALING WITH THE GOVERNMENT

The government of the UAE has made considerable efforts to make it as easy as possible for people to deal with the state, largely through its initiatives with providing e-Government links and portals. A wide range of services and information has been made available online, and this makes things a lot easier for people to prepare themselves for any subsequent interaction. It is advisable for visitors to get to know the relevant information beforehand in any dealing with the government, since a number of business procedures tend to be organized quite differently from the way they are generally handled in other countries, and it is possible for this to lead to disappointment or frustration. An example of this would be government tenders, which, once a would-be contractor has passed the quality thresholds, are usually fiercely negotiated in terms of price. It is not unusual for tender specifications then to be changed and companies asked to re-present their bids accordingly.

The people who work at government service desks, representing departments and utilities, have improved over the years and are generally professional and polite. However, the bureaucracy can nevertheless be opaque and require more paperwork than seems to be necessary, and there can be situations in which it might appear that the service encounter has been unsatisfactory. For example, applying for a visa for another person to visit depends on the discretionary powers of the officer, who will apply them properly but not always in the way that is desired. Similarly, before leaving the country, it is necessary to obtain, complete, and submit a stack of forms to different agencies to demonstrate there will be no unpaid bills left behind. Many find this a tedious process.

WOMEN IN BUSINESS

It is difficult but not impossible for women to do business in the traditional Arab environment. Certain business staples, such as a personal face-to-face meeting, for example, would be very difficult to manage, and issues of status bedevil negotiations. However, in recent years, the UAE government has devoted more effort toward finding employment for its young women, and this will eventually translate into a more convenient business environment for them. The problems that young women face can be considerable: familial and societal prejudice can be very powerful forces, and the fear that a daughter might become unmarriageable would trouble even the most liberal of fathers.

Practical issues also abound. A workplace environment must be found or developed in which the women need not be subject to close contact with men to whom they are not related, either as coworkers or as customers. Apart from ladies' cloakrooms and washing facilities, separate rooms must also be provided for eating, drinking coffee, and praying. Most UAE families have quite well differentiated degrees of freedom that they are prepared to grant to their women, but in practical terms it is necessary to cater to the most conservative parents who are still prepared to let their daughters leave the house and work. Clearly, these restrictions narrow down the fields in which women can work meaningfully and, even if such jobs can be found, there may be little incentive for women to take them because the salary provided is so low compared to family income.

In these circumstances, it is not surprising that private sector companies generally prefer to avoid all the trouble involved and, consequently, it is the government that has stepped in to create jobs suitable for Emirati women. These are commonly found in the Department of Health or Education, and are less likely in commercial or technical departments. Women need to work in a position in which they can remain living in their own home, and it is therefore unusual for them to take a post that might require them to work unsociable hours or involve extensive traveling or overnight stays away. There is, nevertheless, a definite commitment among many parts of the government to obtain more benefit from its female human resources.

Muslim women from other countries working within the UAE generally follow less restrictive regimes, and their role in the business world differs little from that of men, by and large, although physical contact of any sort should still be avoided, unless the woman offers her hand, when it may be briefly touched in lieu of a handshake. Women from Egypt, Iraq, or Jordan or American Arabs may work in the UAE, and their customs vary as their homelands vary. The best thing is to take a cue from the women concerned and be prepared to avoid contact. Visitors also develop the habit of looking around a little more carefully in crowds or public areas such as department stores and shopping malls to avoid accidentally bumping into another person.

Other migrant female workers are frequently placed in the lower ranks of service positions and adapt themselves to local expectations. Western or other women in management positions generally have enough experience to avoid difficult situations, but must nevertheless accustom themselves to what will appear to be the occasional snub or insult. Even when the business situation is not dominated by Arab customs, much of the business world is in any case dominated by the rather macho oil exploration industry and by the preponderance of male migrant workers, and so may be less sympathetic to the concept of women in the working world. This will have an effect upon the way in which socialization after work hours is managed.

chapter nine

COMMUNICATING

Cross-cultural communication can be difficult because of the different meanings and values people from different cultures attach to the same objects. Just take one example: a tent. In the UAE a tent is a large and sometimes ornate structure with internal partitions, which is strongly associated with the past and with the ancient tribal and familial rural histories that are sentimentalized in many societies; it is also, today, a portable item that represents convenience and comfort in difficult surroundings. This is very different from what it means to most foreigners, who regard it as a primitive form of shelter, and possibly inadequate protection in a dangerous environment. Similarly separate meanings are also given to important cultural icons, such as ships, camels, and the desert itself.

Words that denote complex and contested

concepts, such as "freedom," "sacred," or "responsibility," can diverge greatly from culture to culture. Try not to judge people who may hold different understandings of what these things mean, and instead listen to what they say and try to understand it. This does not mean that the visitor should accept or believe everything that is heard, but just that it should be judged on its own merits. For example, attitudes to the role of women can vary significantly from country to country and culture to culture: each society more or less believes that the way it does things is, if not perfect, then probably right. Listening to Emiratis, men and women alike, speaking about the appropriate role of women in society without automatically judging them can reveal new ways of thinking about the issues involved; even if you ulimately reject their views, the exercise in empathy will help you to reflect on your own personal beliefs and perhaps lead to a deeper appreciation of them.

What all this signifies is, of course, that one should keep as open a mind as possible when interacting with the people of the UAE. By all means, the visitor should maintain personal beliefs and ideologies, but only when these have been carefully and honestly scrutinized in the light of what the Emiratis believe.

LANGUAGE

The Arabic language spoken by the Emirati population is, according to Islamic belief, sacred because it was the language God used to give the Koran to the world. That means that any insult to the language is deeply bound up with an insult to the religion people feel to be very close to the purpose of their lives. Jokes or puns that are possible in other languages are not possible in Arabic to outsiders; at the same time, poets and

lyricists are free within limits to juxtapose and reimagine language in a view toward artistic and perhaps spiritual re-creation of reality.

If the Arabic language is given by God, then words and names have deep, deep meanings that should not be abused. Many visitors find difficulty in understanding this and, to deal with the problem, become inarticulate or reticent in company. This is understandable because it is difficult to appreciate the perspective of another culture without either reflexively repudiating it or else just accepting everything as a reasonably valid alternative view of the world. Humanity has yet to resolve this issue, and the visitor to the UAE should not feel in any way inadequate for being unable to do any better.

Written Arabic is read from right to left, which is initially counter-intuitive for many visitors until it is practiced for a while. There is only one sound in the Arabic language that is not also used in English or most Romance languages, which is the guttural sound of the letter Ayn, "argh," usually represented in foreign language by a colon (:). This is a commonly heard sound. According to linguists, the way of producing some of the consonant sounds in Arabic is different from the ways used in Western languages but, in practice, the sounds are similar enough for differences to be ignored, at least for the foreigner. As a country with what is now quite a highly educated people, the form of Arabic spoken and written in the UAE is quite strongly influenced by classical Arabic. The diversity of Arabic spoken across the Arab world, especially in terms of conversational and colloquial forms of the language, is such that there are some dialects that cannot be mutually understood. Most Arabic-speaking visitors in the UAE will try to adapt their style and vocabulary to local usage when interacting with Emirati people. The spread of television and other forms of mass media using Arabic has also helped to stabilize a general level of understanding of all Arabic speakers, even if they retain their own dialects in personal conversations.

Arabic nouns and adjectives are introduced by the definite article, *al*, in which the consonant sound is occasionally modified by a succeeding consonant. For example, the name Al al-din is usually pronounced Aladdin (the "d" being pronounced twice). Many English words beginning with *al* sounds show their origins in Arabic: these include arithmetic, algorithm, algebra, and Africa. In the pre-modern age, Arabic thought and philosophy were highly advanced, and led the world in areas such as hygiene, medicine, and mathematics.

The basic form of a word in Arabic is three consonants, which are customarily linked by two internal vowels, although some variations are possible. The choice of vowel determines the precise meaning of the word: e.g., book, library, student, and so forth are based on the same three consonants (*ktb*). Words may be modified by particles placed on their ends, to make plurals or denote ownership, although these tend to be less commonly employed than they once were. Verbs also adopt similar patterns in terms of construction, as do nouns and adjectives, but are modified by initial and ending particles. For example, the nouns *muslameen wa muslimaat* mean Muslim men and Muslim women (that is, the Islamic world). The modifiers generally appear at the end of the sentence. Vowels appear above or below the consonants, and there are some additional aspiration marks. Pronunciation is phonetic.

Owing to its divine provenance and the fact that Islamic thought frowns upon the depiction of human beings, Arabic calligraphy is often used as a form of art, generally devotional in nature. It may be found inscribed on plates and other decorations, and these should be treated respectfully. Indeed, it is advisable to treat any written or printed material with care, in case it contains any kind of religious message. Certainly, it is important to avoid touching such literature with the foot or shoes.

POLITE BEHAVIOR

As we have seen, it is easy to cause offense by making a comment that might be construed as an insult to the Arabic language, or straying into sensitive national, cultural, and religious issues. Of course, this in part depends on the willingness of another person to take offense, particularly when it may be clear that none was intended.

A great deal of humor in Western culture is based on word play, and this does not translate well into the UAE, unless dealing with someone with considerable international experience and an open mind. Self-deprecating humor also does not translate very well. In general, it is advisable to speak plainly and clearly, avoiding too many verbal flourishes, metaphors, and similes. These are particularly tricky because it is common in most Western languages to anthropomorphize animals or inanimate objects, perhaps in order to make some humorous point, for example by comparing a person to an animal like a faithful dog or a hardworking ox. This is something that may cause offense because it likens a human being, whose shape and nature has been dictated by God, with a lesser item or creature.

In other cases, normal conversational manners of course also apply in the UAE. Avoid interrupting people who are older or of higher status—which necessarily means being always aware of personal social status and the relative status of all those involved. Although this may require some concentration initially, it becomes intuitive after a short period. Visitors should generally permit other people to speak for as long as they wish and to be encouraged to speak more if they give the impression that they may wish to do so. Arabic culture places a great deal of emphasis on consensus as a means of reaching decisions, and this can only really be achieved when everyone believes he or she has made such contribution as is desired.

This concept also has an impact upon the managerial style that a visitor should adopt when dealing with Emirati people. Abruptly made, opaque decisions are unlikely to be welcomed if they are foisted on people who do not have the opportunity to have their say. Of course, this form of consensus reaching can be time-consuming and, for those not accustomed to it, might appear to be inefficient. Nevertheless, it is an important part of communication and should be used wherever possible.

The protocol of meetings and other social gatherings dictates that before settling down to the main events of the agenda suitable refreshments should be offered and various (nonspecific) conversational topics be discussed. These include establishing who is related to whom and who has what history. Visitors should follow the example of their Emirati hosts at meetings or gatherings, without of course assuming the role of host.

THE COMMUNICATIONS REVOLUTION

The UAE is now a modern society with strong access to integrated mobile and Internet technology, provided by the state-owned company Etisalat. This company generally offers a good service, although of course it is always possible to find some people whose experience of any company has been unsatisfactory in one way or another. Where visitors to the UAE are likely to be dissatisfied is in access to certain Web sites and services. Owing to cultural and to security concerns, a large number of such Web sites are blocked; sometimes these are for obvious reasons because the material they carry is judged objectionable or obscene or otherwise inappropriate. In other cases, the blocking removes access to other connected sites that might be wholly blameless or in other cases blocked apparently by accident or mistake—or more likely for a reason that is not immediately obvious to the Web surfer. It is best to come to terms with this quite early, as  Etisalat rarely changes its mind about these decisions and, in any case, there are so many resources available on the Internet that it is not difficult to find alternatives in nearly all cases.

Cinema and home watching of movies via VCD or DVD are also widely available and popular. The choice of movies is affected by the suitability of the content, as is also true of the many cinemas in the country, which are customarily very pleasant and often nearly empty, unless there is a major opening.

In common with other societies, the ways that young people in particular communicate with each other is being affected by the use of modern communication devices, specifically cell phones and their texting functions, as well as Internet applications. These change and mutate so rapidly that it is hardly worth trying to record them. Young people are usually able to pick up the proper usage, while older people tend not to be so capable. The strong taboos in place against unmarried men and women meeting each other are being modified by the use of cell phones, since people can send messages to each other or use Bluetooth technology to beep one another so as to initiate and sustain conversations at a chaste distance. Women wearing full *abaya* and *shayla* can use their cell phones discreetly with hands-free kits without anyone knowing what they are doing.

THE MEDIA

The media industry has developed considerably in recent years. Now there are numerous newspapers, magazines, television channels, and radio stations, and UAE institutions have strong online presences. The UAE government recognized that there is space in the media world for an authentic, modern voice for the Arab and, more broadly, the Muslim world. The commercial and political success of the Al Jazeera television station, based in Qatar, bears testament to the demand for such a voice. Resources have been placed behind local media outlets, especially in Dubai, to provide this national voice with some success.

A variety of newspapers and magazines caters to different segments of the local population. News coverage is slanted toward the particular interest of the target market, offering extended coverage of South Asia, the Western world, or other places accordingly. Much of the news coverage is syndicated, to reduce costs, which means it is the same information that appears in most newspapers around the world. They are generally cheap and of reasonable quality. Visitors who are interested in contributing to the local media outlets are likely to find a welcome from editors, who in the UAE as everywhere else, are involved in a constant search for good content.

Radio and television are freely available, with a range of cable services to which subscriptions may be made. Again, should cable feeds contain objectionable material this is likely to be summarily censored or removed. This also includes advertisements that are contracted for another geographical region but not for the UAE, or that are restricted in the UAE. Most services are quite stable and are not often lost because of transmission difficulties in the atmosphere, though this has happened in the past. Local television services offer a range of news and programs, principally in Arabic and English. Ethnic minorities also have some programs of particular interest, provided either locally or by subscription from overseas. The same applies to radio stations, which offer a range of programs, although they tend toward the populist. The population of the UAE is comparatively small and fragmented into many diverse groups, based on ethnicity, hence the audience size is small for individual stations. Licenses are offered to stations on a commercial basis and so advertisements generally appear on all feeds. Radio stations have a tendency to close down after their yearly license expires if they are not making money. To reduce costs, many are now automated with computer-generated playlists and no DJs on the premises.

CONCLUSION

The UAE is a country facing both the past and the future. There is a genuine and deep respect in most people for the traditions and cultural practices of the past, even as society speeds into a future in which those traditions are left far behind. Emirati men and women proudly wear their traditional clothing while at the same time using the most advanced technology for wireless communications with their friends, families, and colleagues. This image of joint tradition and modernity is a good one for the country, and visitors might use it to help dispel superficial assumptions about the way that people are, how they behave, and what they think. Adherence to traditional beliefs and religious faith does not preclude sophistication and complex methods of thought. Nor is it the case that maintaining a religious philosophy and following its observances necessarily makes a person think that other ways of life are always inferior or invalid. Many Emiratis understand and accept alternative forms of living and thinking, and see their good points and bad points without wishing to change their own perspectives. Since their own standard of living exceeds that of most other countries, moreover, the people of the UAE have little motivation to aspire to another form of lifestyle or feel aspirations to achieve it. The upshot of this is that it is prudent for the visitor to the UAE to have a slightly humble approach and be hesitant about suggesting that things might be better elsewhere or that there are problems with the way in which UAE society is organized.

Change is being embraced by UAE society, and there is a national vision to which most subscribe that sees the country as being a leader of the Arab world and an example of how a faithful religious society can also be a

forward-looking one. With a modern
economy, built by oil but preparing for life
and growth when it runs out, and a tolerant
and forgiving approach to the international
world, the UAE represents a model society for
the Arab world in the future. The Emirati
people themselves embody this combination
of past and present in a fascinating way. In a
time of accelerating change, their open and
measured approach to balancing ancient and
modern values is an example to which many
parts of the developing world could aspire.

Further Reading

Armstrong, Karen. *Muhammad: A Prophet for Our Time.* San Francisco: HarperSanFrancisco, 2007.

Brustad, Kristen, Mahmoud al-Batal, and Abbas al-Tonsi. *Al-kitaab fii Ta'allum Al-'Arabiyya with DVDs* (A Textbook for Beginning Arabic). Washington, DC: Georgetown University Press, 2004.

Damluji, Salma S., ed. *The Architecture of the United Arab Emirates.* Reading, UK: Ithaca Press, 2006.

Davidson, Christopher M. *The United Arab Emirates: A Study in Survival.* London: Lynne Rienner Publishers, 2005.

Esposito, John L., ed. *The Oxford History of Islam.* Oxford: Oxford University Press, 2000.

Heard-Bey, Frauke. *From Trucial States to United Arab Emirates.* London and New York: Longman, 1997.

Hoyland, Robert. *Arabia and the Arabs: From the Bronze Age to the Coming of Islam.* London: Routledge, 2001.

Hurriez, Sayyid. *Folklore and Folklife in the United Arab Emirates.* New York: RoutledgeCurzon, 2002.

Rugh, Andrea B. *The Political Culture of Leadership in the United Arab Emirates.* New York: Palgrave Macmillan, 2007.

Zahlan, Rosemarie Said. *The Origins of the United Arab Emirates: A Political and Social History of the Trucial States.* New York: Palgrave Macmillan, 1978.

Complete Arabic: The Basics. New York: Living Languge, 2005.

In-Flight Arabic. New York: Living Language, 2001.

Useful Web Sites

The starting point for interaction with the e-Government of the UAE may be found at: www.government.ae/gov/en/index.jsp

Transparency International has a Web site at: www.transparency.org

culture smart! uae

Index